Fr. Paul Trinchard, S.T.L.

THE MASS
That MADE PADRE PIO

Published by

MAETA
METAIRIE LOUISIANA

Padre Pio Cover & Drawings: Barbara Kellam

Cover Design: Karen M. Albert

Manuscript Preparation: Elizabeth Allen

Published by MAETA

Printed in the United States of America

Library of Congress Catalog Number: 96-76325

ISBN 1-889168-01-7

Padre Pio on Cover: Barbara Kellam

TERMS

STIGMATA, marks said to have been supernaturally impressed upon the bodies of certain persons in imitation of the wounds on the crucified body of Christ (the stigmata of St. Francis). (The New Webster Encyclopedic Dictionary of the English Language, Consolidated Book Publishers, Chicago, 1980)

Briefly, *stigmata* is defined as that phenomena in which a person bears all or some of the wounds of Christ...which appear spontaneously from no external source, with a periodic flow of fresh blood...generally recurring on the days... associated with Christ's Passion...do not yield to the usual medical treatment...may remain for 30 to 40 years...is preceded and attended by keen physical and moral sufferings...found only in persons who practice heroic virtues and possess a devout and special love of the Cross. (Pocket Catholic Dictionary, John A. Hardon, S.J., Image Books)

STIGMATIC, one who possesses such marks, as described above.

CRUCIFIED

Our cover here depicts Padre Pio carrying the crucifix. The crucifix represents both Christ-Crucified and Padre Pio as conforming to Christ-Crucified. In these anti-Catholic times, each of us must be reminded that we are to conform to Christ-Crucified. The present obsession on living Christ-glorified is both unreal and blasphemous. Consider now the words of St. Louis De Montfort.

> You take pride in being God's children and you do well; but you should also rejoice in the lashes your good Father has given you and in those He still means to give you; for He scourges every one of His children (Prov 3,22; Heb 13, 5-6; Apoc 3, 19). If you are not of the household of His beloved sons, then-- how unfortunate! What a calamity! You are, as St. Augustine says, listed with the reprobate.

Ultimately, each of us is either of this

world or of Heaven. Augustine says: 'The one that does not mourn like a stranger and wayfarer in this world cannot rejoice in the world to come as a citizen of heaven' (Sermon 31, 5-6). If God the Father does not send you worthwhile crosses from time to time, that is because He no longer cares for you and is angry at you. He considers you a stranger, an outsider undeserving of His hospitality, or an unlawful child who has no right to share in his father's estate and no title to his father's supervision and discipline.

Friends of the Cross, disciples of a crucified God, the mystery of the Cross is a mystery unknown to the Gentiles, repudiated by the Jews and spurned by both heretics and bad Catholics, yet it is the great mystery which you must learn only at His school. (St. Louis De Montfort)

THE MASS THAT MADE PADRE PIO

TABLE OF CONTENTS

THE MASS THAT MADE PADRE PIO

TABLE OF CONTENTS

FORWARD

Francisco Forgione was born on May 25, 1887. Padre (Father) Pio is his Capuchin religious name. He chose to name himself after the pope-saint of the Canonized Mass--Pope Saint Pius V. The Canonized Mass was the only Mass Padre Pio ever said. He said it with such priestly fervor that it lasted for three or more hours every day.

Padre Pio was the *first*--the first stigmatist-priest, the first priest to manifest in his own body, the Mass he was privileged to celebrate. He was the *last*--the last and most sensational sacerdotal fruit of that Mass which would be (temporarily, we pray) "outlawed" during the final months of Padre Pio's life.

Having suffered in Christ, even to the shedding of all of his blood, our popularly acclaimed saint, Padre Pio, died on September 23, 1968. Did God manifest Padre Pio--the only stigmatist-priest in Church history--as the best fruit of the Canonized Mass Liturgy right before its (temporary) eclipse? Recall that Padre Pio's stigmata occurred *after* he became a priest--*after* he said the Canonized Mass. Was the stigmata *uniquely* bestowed upon this priest because he said, prayed and conformed to the Holy Sacrifice as few, if any priests before him, ever did.

Through Padre Pio's intercession, will not the Canonized Mass flourish again? Through the intercession of this saint of the Canonized Mass Liturgy may each reader be led to a deeper understanding of the Canonized Mass--the Mass that made Padre Pio. May these Mass prayers which made Padre Pio, inspire and strengthen us and, we pray, motivate and enable many young men to become special children of Padre Pio--*priests*--like unto him.

Fr. Paul Trinchard

ORDAINED TO BLESS
CHALLENGED TO BE BLESSED

When pronouncing the words of Consecration, he [Padre Pio, the Saint of the Canonized Mass] seems to suffer a real martyrdom; as he raises the consecrated Host and Chalice with every appearance of tenderest love and deepest adoration, little streams of blood are seen trickling from the wounds on his hands. Those who assist at one of Padre Pio's Masses...know what the Mass really is...a repetition of the Sacrifice of Calvary. (The Two Stigmatists Padre Pio and Teresa Neumann, Rev. Charles M. Carty, The Radio Replies Press Society, St. Paul, 1956)

In Sacred Scripture, whenever God *blesses in the fullness of His power,* He destroys and salutarily creates or recreates. We perceive God doing this in Genesis (Gn 1:1-3). He destroyed some of the *"chaos, waste, cursed"* and created light which was salutary or good (in the full meaning of the text). He destroyed some of the *evil* and created *good* or *salvation.*

Padre Pio, other priests and I myself, who were ordained before 1969, were explicitly given the *"Christ-power to bless"*--power from God the Father to *bless into being Christ-Sacrifice and Sacrament.* We were given the power to destroy bread and wine and create Christ salutarily present among us. Here are the pertinent words from ordinations before 1969:

> *Theirs be the task to change with* **blessing undefiled...***bread and wine into the Body and Blood of Thy Son.* (The old Ordinal on the nature of the Orders conferred)

This prayer defined Padre Pio as a Catholic priest. He was Christ-priest, who blessed with *blessing undefiled* bread and wine into Christ. This unique blessing-power was explicitly given to him (and all validly ordained priests) by God the Father through his valid ordination to the priesthood. Indeed, his ordination defined Padre Pio. With what devotion, he must have recalled and meditated upon that day of his metamorphasis, his own blessing through which he died as an ordinary Catholic and was created Christ-priest. The following ritual by which Padre Pio was ordained has been discarded.

> The *Veni Creator Spiritus* was intoned while his bishop anointed Padre Pio's hands. Dipping his right thumb into the oil of the Catechumens he anointed his opened hands in the form of a cross by tracing two lines, one from the thumb of the right hand to the index finger of the left, the other from the thumb of the left hand to the corresponding finger of the right. He then anointed Padre Pio's palms all over. In doing so he said:
>
> *Be pleased, Lord, to consecrate and sanctify these hands by this anointing, and our blessing.* Then he made the sign of the cross over Padre Pio's outstretched hands, made explicit and confirmed Padre Pio's being *ordained to bless: **That whatsoever they bless may be blessed...consecrated and sanctified in the name of Our Lord Jesus Christ.***

Padre Pio, the first priest-stigmatist, lived up to his ordination challenge outstandingly. He knew and imitated Jesus Christ, Whom as Christ-priest, he *blessed into being*. He became more *like unto Christ* than any other priest we know. He, more than any other priest, spectacularly lived up to his ordination commission, *the commission to be blessed*:

> *Agnosce ergo quod agis, imitare quod tractas, quatenus, mortis et resurrectionis Domini mysterium celebrans, membra tua a vitiis omnibus mortificare et in novitate vitae ambulare studeas.*(Padre Pio's ordination challenge)

> *Come to realize ever more fully your Christ-priest power to bless.Become ever more aware of who you now are. Imitate Whom you bless into being and 'handle.' As you exercise your Christ-priest power, celebrating the sacred mystery of the passion, death and resurrection of Our Lord and Saviour, mortify your entire self so that Christ Whom you bring into being at your Masses, may come to 'fully be' in you: now as dying and eternally, as risen.*
> (Padre Pio's ordination challenge as given in the old Ordinal)

This book will give you a proper and profitable picture of this priest who was *ordained to bless* and *challenged to be blessed.* He is the example for all priests who were similarly ordained. Indeed, more than any other priest, Padre Pio became the mystic stigmatist that he was *because of his becoming "Padre."* As such, he was *ordained to bless* (to metamorphasize) bread and wine into Christ--Sacrifice and Sacrament; and with God's special graces bestowed upon him in Holy Orders, he lived up to his special ordination challenge to be *blessed into being an "alter Christus."*

DEDICATED TO THE HOLY PIO TRIO

Lex orandi, lex credendi. This truth is now evident and will become more visibly manifested every day until the new era of ecclesial reparation materializes--until the pre-dawn darkness brings on a bright and glorious tomorrow. *As one prays, one believes; and, as one believes, so one prays.*

Holy Pio Quinto (Pope St. Pius V) papally and dogmatically canonized the Mass liturgy (for the Latin Rite) for all times and places. He did so *to preserve the one and only true religion.*

Holy Pio Decimo (Pope St. Pius X) dogmatically condemned the mega-heresy which has now invaded the ecclesial establishment. He did so *to preserve the Canonized Mass--the one and only Salutary Deed and Presence among us. Lex orandi, lex credendi.*

Holy Padre Pio was the most spectacular fruit of this Canonized Mass. *This and only this Mass liturgy (which was canonized by Pio Quinto--Pius*

V) *produced Padre Pio.* Also, Padre Pio fulfilled the expectations of his namesake, Pio Quinto (Pius V) and Pio Decimo (Pius X), for in praying the Canonized Mass, Padre Pio came to believe in and live the true Faith as few others have ever done.

> *Holy Pio Trio--St. Pius V, St. Pius X and Padre Pio, pray for us who live in this age of unprecedented fiducial and liturgical darkness. May the Light of Christ, through the intercession of the Immaculata, the Holy Pio Trio and all other saints, break through the present darkness to enlighten, empower and enliven us. May faith and liturgical morals come to flourish among us as in previous times.*

CHAPTER ONE

BRIEF BIOGRAPHY

Francisco Forgione, born on May 25, 1887, was baptized when he was less than a day old. Less than one month after his ordination to the priesthood, on August 10, 1910, he received the *invisible* stigmata. Then, some eight years later, he received the *visible* stigmata.

Padre Pio suffered the phenomenon of transverberation. By definition, transverberation means the piercing of the heart by an angel. Padre underwent this great suffering on the evening of August 5, 1918, while hearing confessions.

He was wounded in the heart by a celestial angel as with a long, sharp, pointed blade which seemed to emit fire. He experienced such agony that he was forced to retire in dreadful pain, which lasted until the morning of August 7. His heart had been lacerated and even his viscera were torn. Padre

Pio related in detail this mystical phenomenon in a letter to Padre Benedetto. (Letter No. 500, August 21, 1918) On September 20, 1918, Padre Pio received the visible stigmata, which he suffered for fifty years. At the beginning, the visible stigmata were small wounds, but after several months, they became large and round, having a diameter of two centimeters.

The wound on his side had the form of a cross, (caused by receiving *both* transverberation and the stigmata) the lower part of which slanted from the fifth rib to the ninth, while the cross-bar was about half as long.   Other well-known attributes of Padre Pio included his numerous instances of bi-location, and charismatic aromas, indicating the manner in which Padre Pio follows souls who seek his intercession; as well as his performing numerous miracles.

In addition to the stigmata and transverberation, he suffered the crowning with thorns and the scourging. The only other known instance of the mystical phenomenon of transverberation occurred in St. Theresa of Avila. Indeed, there are

2

many other prodigious aspects of Padre Pio as a stigmatist and mystic. Among other physical sufferings of Padre Pio were his prolonged and mysterious illnesses. Scientists were perplexed, of course, to learn that very often his body temperature reached 110 degrees Fahrenheit or higher. Temperatures above 107 degrees are normally fatal.

When Padre Pio died on September 23, 1968, according to his personal physician, Doctor Sala, his body was bloodless. He had shed all of his blood for Christ. His five wounds *healed* in his death (not before, nor after) as recorded in the medical report of his death and the testimony of many eye witnesses.

For three months before his death, he bled less and less. His body was in the process of shedding its last drops of blood. At the time of his death, the surfaces became covered with a thin layer of skin.

The sworn testimony of doctors and others, confirms this as fact. Their testimony revealed that using a light, one could still see through the wounds. Therefore, there was no tissue regeneration within the wounds, but only at the surface.

The material that will lead to Padre Pio's canonization already fills over twenty-three volumes. Seldom before has any saint accumulated so much evidence for his sanctity in such a short time.

Salvation isn't a *once and forever finished* affair. No! Each can easily lose salvation from Hell, which was given by the waters of a valid Baptism. The road to salvation is narrow and arduous. Few complete it. Such a salutary condition is confirmed as one prays the *Hail Mary.*

> *Holy Mary, Mother of God, pray for us sinners, now and at the hour of our death?*

Each of us will be judged by Jesus. Each needs all the help he can get to avoid going to eternal Hell. Many will go to eternal Hell for post-Baptismal sins.

In order to escape the fires of Hell, adults must die to their natural desires (the flesh) and the expectations of men (the world). They must dies and be reborn. Padre Pio attests to this in his own life. In his writings, he refers to his own purgation--active and passive.

> The Father wanted to detach his son from innocent and childish loves...from all that is of clay...He allowed those who

were attached to this earth to mistreat me and to be ungrateful that I might understand how false and mistaken is that love I bestowed upon created things...After I understood such ugliness and wretchedness, God invited me to a different life. (Padre Pio, Letters, vol. 3, p. 251)

REPARATION FOR SIN
LIVE THE MASS AS PADRE PIO DID

The Canonized Mass has always been loved by holy people. Padre Pio loved this Mass. He not only said the Canonized Mass, he prayed and lived the Mass in a way no other priest has ever done. This saying, praying, and living, by itself and in itself, defined and produced Padre Pio.

As Padre Pio disclosed to us--if he could, he would say the Mass every moment of his life. The Mass was the love of his life. The Mass was his life! Each of us who are blessed with an adequate understanding of the Canonized Mass can easily perceive that the Mass is the continual, essential and fundamental ingredient in the formation, sustenance, motivation and identity of Padre Pio.

The more one comes to see and appreciate the Canonized Mass, the more one comes to appreciate Padre Pio. The more one comes to see and appreciate Padre Pio, the more one comes to understand and appreciate the Canonized Mass Liturgy. The more one follows Padre Pio--the *only stigmatic priest* in the history of Catholicism--the more one comes to resemble or conform to Padre Pio, the most spectacular *product of the Canonized Mass Liturgy of the Latin Rite of the Roman Catholic Church.*

PADRE PIO
ANTIDOTE TO POPULAR HERESY

By *living the Mass*, Padre Pio refuted a basic popular heresy. We are not saved *past tense.* We are saved *active tense.* Being baptized and embracing Catholicism is just the beginning of our arduous trip down the narrow road. Few finish this trip. Few go to Heaven (Mt 7:14). Few conform to Christ Crucified.

We are not sinless Risen Christs whose only task is to perfect ourselves and this world. We are to be graced sinners, dedicated to, and actually walking the narrow path with broken bodies like unto Christ's broken Body, all the while shedding our life-blood through, and in union with, Christ, Who shed His Blood for our sins.

The realities of the Canonized Mass--the Saving Person and the Saving Event--defined Padre Pio. He became who he was because he said, prayed, loved and lived the one and only Canonized Mass Liturgy of the Latin Rite of the Catholic Church.

By God's providence, Padre Pio lived and died, having said only the Canonized Mass. We know that at least since 1960, Padre Pio suffered such bad eyesight that he obtained permission from Rome to use the Votive Mass of our Blessed Mother or the Mass for the Dead. As he aged, his vision worsened. Therefore, quite logically, he could not see nor memorize any entirely new liturgy.

CHAPTER THREE

OUR LADY OF THE CANONIZED MASS

Anyone who is devoted to the Canonized Mass will inevitably be devoted to Our Lady and vice versa. This truth was exemplified in Padre Pio. Between Masses, he *bonded* with Our Lady by saying many rosaries every day. At Mass, he was conscious of the special presence of the Co-Redemptrix--Christ's *first and best-loved* rational creation. For many years toward the end of his life, his increasing blindness led him to gain permission to say the Mass of the Immaculata.

Mary is Our Lady of the *Canonized* or *Tridentine* Mass. All of Our Lady's Church approved apparitions were linked to the Canonized Mass-- the Mass that made Padre Pio. All of Our Lady's popular visitations commanded that a chapel be built for the Canonized Mass and to provide a place for her Child to tabernacle among us. Is this not what we would expect from Christ's loving Mother?

The Canonized Mass--and only the Canonized

Mass--*was* said in all such chapels. The Canonized Mass is Mary's Mass. Only the Canonized Mass was instituted by Christ for the Latin Rite. We note that recent Marian signs are negative. Our Lady is displeased. Her messages have been ignored, distorted and vilified--especially, by the upper clergy. Does Mary weep over the fact that the Christ-instituted Mass that made Padre Pio is no longer respected, nor available for her children?

Our Lady, as Co-Redemptrix, suffered and was herself crucified at Calvary through, with and in her Son, Jesus. Therefore, Our Lady has a special relationship to each valid Mass. Each such Mass is the Unbloody Sacrifice of Calvary--the one and only *so great Salvation* (Hb 2:3).

OUR LADY OF THE CANONIZED MASS
OUR LADY OF GUADALUPE

In 1531, Our Lady appeared as Our Lady of the Apocalypse (Apoc 12). She appeared clothed with the sun (Apoc 12:1). Her black ribbon indicated she was with Child (Apoc 12:2). She came to defeat Satan (Apoc 12:3). She would defeat Satan by the Holy Sacrifice and the Holy Sacrament.

What was her message? Our Lady requested that a *traditional or canonical chapel* be built to help bring her Child's Canonized Sacrifice of the Mass to the Americas and to tabernacle her Child among us. So far, Our Lady hasn't withdrawn her miraculous portrait from the mid-American shrine within which the Canonized Mass is no longer said.

Apparently, she patiently waits for the restoration of the Holy Sacrifice of the Mass--that Liturgy which she miraculously and clearly requested to be said in 1531--that same Christ-instituted liturgy which made Padre Pio the only stigmatist-priest in the history of Catholicism. Indeed, she patiently waits for that day and season when once again the Canonized Mass will be celebrated at her shrine and throughout the Catholic world, as it was during the lifetime of Padre Pio.

OUR LADY OF THE CANONIZED MASS
OUR LADY OF FRANCE

It isn't coincidental that the celebration of the Canonized Mass is more prevalent in France than anywhere else. Of those who attend a "Catholic" liturgy regularly on Sundays, *a significant number* attend the Canonized Mass.

Our Lady blessed France with the greatest number of major Marian apparitions of modern times. In a special way, France is loved by Our Lady.

Beginning in Paris at Rue du Bac, St. Catherine Laboure, in 1830, received the Miraculous Medal from the Immaculata in the sanctuary of this chapel. In this sanctuary, as in the sanctuary where Padre Pio said his Masses--the Holy Sacrifice and the Holy Sacrament came into man's space and time.

OUR LADY OF THE CANONIZED MASS
OUR LADY OF LA SALETTE

> Priests by their evil lives, by their irreverences and impiety *in celebrating the Holy Mysteries*...have become sewers of impurity. (Our Lady of La Salette, 1846)

Our Lady appeared to Maximin Giraud (age 11) and Melanie Calvat (age 15). At La Salette, Our Lady wept. She focused on the main danger facing us--unworthy or evil priests, bishops and popes and *our* putting *them* before and in place of God and His Salutary Will. Our Lady *wept*.

Our Lady disclosed that there will come a time when bishops and popes will become dysfunctional and demonic. Even Rome will become corrupt.

> **Rome will lose the Faith and become the seat of anti-christ...The Church will be in *eclipse.***

Melanie was uniquely bonded to the Holy Sacrifice and Holy Sacrament. She lived for long

15

periods without food. *Her only food was the Fruit of the Holy Sacrifice*--the Holy Eucharist.

OUR LADY OF THE CANONIZED MASS
OUR LADY OF LOURDES

What was the message to St. Bernadette in 1858? *Build a chapel here*! Build a chapel for the celebration of the Canonized Mass--that Mass which made Padre Pio. Thus will Christ come to dwell with you in a special way and to bless you. As always, Our Lady leads us to her Son and His Holy Sacrifice of Mass in our very midst.

OUR LADY OF THE CANONIZED MASS
OUR LADY OF KNOCK

On August 21, 1879, Our Lady, St. Joseph and St. John appeared in the Church in County Mayo, Ireland. They appeared within the Mass--with the *crucifix* and the Altar of the Lamb. The Lamb of the Apocalypse defines Heaven (Apoc 4). This is the Sacrificed Lamb of the Canonized Mass. This is the Mass done eternally in Heaven. This is the Mass which we pray will always be done on earth in like manner.

This shrine was approved by the Holy See. It is frequented by over a million visitors each year. Here, Our Lady of the Canonized Mass is honored. Unfortunately, the Mass she specifically *apparitioned* is no longer celebrated at Knock. Here, as in other shrines of Our Lady of the Canonized Mass--the Canonized Mass is outlawed. No wonder she weeps.

OUR LADY OF THE CANONIZED MASS
OUR LADY OF FATIMA

Most Holy Trinity, Father, Son and Holy Ghost, I adore Thee profoundly. I offer Thee the Most Precious Body, Blood, Soul and Divinity of Thy Most Beloved Son, Our Lord and Saviour Jesus Christ, present in all the tabernacles throughout the world, in reparation for all the outrages, sacrileges and indifferences by which He Himself is offended. And

17

through the infinite merits of His Most Sacred Heart and the intercession of the Immaculate Heart of Mary, I pray for the conversion of poor sinners. (Eucharistic prayer given at Fatima).

We tend to forget that the Holy Eucharist--*from a Canonized Mass*--was the first focus of God's Fatima Message. During 1916, the children were led to adore the Holy Eucharist; to offer the Holy Eucharist in reparation for sin; and, to center their lives on the Canonized Mass, wherein the Holy Sacrament is consecrated. I personally believe that this *Holy Eucharist* came from one of Padre Pio's Masses.

St. John Bosco's vision of the Holy Eucharist and Our Lady demonstrated that *these* should be the two pillars of our lives. The Holy Eucharist and Our Lady are inseparable--as they were in the life of our saint--Padre Pio. Our Lady *is* Our Lady of the Canonized Mass and thus Our Lady of the Eucharist. She is the Mother of Jesus. Therefore, she is the Mother of God.

In accord with the Colossians' Mystery, Mary

18

was instrumental in the salvation of the Elect. In accord with who she was, Mary was *the human person involved in the salvation of the Elect*--as St. Maximilian Kolbe emphasized.

What is another message of Fatima? It is b*uild a chapel here*--a chapel within which the Canonized Mass is to be said.

What liturgy is *forbidden at Fatima?* The Canonized Mass Liturgy is forbidden at Fatima. The Fatima situation typifies our problem. Our problem is the wickedness of the upper clergy. Padre Pio, allegedly and appropriately disclosed the Third Revelation of Fatima in these simple words: *"Beware of the bishops!"*

Has not the present liturgical crisis been brought on by *uncorrected bishops?* Are we not in dire need of Padre Pio's intercession to conquer the bishops' rebellion and to repare the Church--especially, to restore the Christ-instituted Holy Sacrifice of the Mass, the Mass that made Padre Pio?

CHAPTER FOUR

THE LAST MARIAN THEOPHANY

Padre Pio had an intense devotion to Our Lady of Fatima. Within the monastery was a shrine to her--a large picture of Our Lady of Fatima, surrounded by burning candles. Each day, Padre Pio would kneel and pray at this oratory.

We cannot understand and appreciate the stigmatist-priest without understanding and appreciating the Fatima Message. He embraced it. He lived it. In doing so, he manifested the Fatima Message. The Fatima Message concerns salvation from Hell unto Heaven. Therefore, the apparitions of Fatima, both explicitly and implicitly focused on the Mass and the Holy Eucharist.

Three elements constitute each Mass--acknowledging God as objectively revealed; confessing ourselves as Hell-bound sinners; and seeking salvation and sanctification through Jesus Christ, Sacrifice and Sacrament. We see these elements in the apparitions of Fatima--the apparitions of the angel in 1916 and in Our Lady's messages in 1917. Throughout this book, we will see this message *incarnated in Padre Pio*.

As if to give to us her last will and testament for this generation, Our Lady left us as the climax of the Fatima Message--the salutary theophany at Tuy. This theophany, perhaps the greatest theophany concerning the Holy Mass, was given to us at Tuy in 1929--while Padre Pio was a priest who celebrated this Holy Sacrifice of the Mass. This theophany, or God's revelation to mankind, occurred at Tuy, Spain, where Sister Lucy of Fatima had a vision far more spectacular than the theophany to Moses on Mount Sinai and comparable to God's theophany (the Transfiguration) to his selected apostles on Mount Tabor.

On June 13, 1929, Sister Lucy of Fatima experienced this salutary theophany. She left us a brief description of this, her God-given mystical interpretation of the Holy Sacrifice. Before the Blessed Sacrament, which was born of the Holy Sacrifice, she recited, again and again, the Mass-centered prayers given to her by God's angel in 1916, at Fatima, Portugal.

Suddenly a supernatural light illumined the whole chapel and on the altar appeared a cross of light which reached to the ceiling. In a brighter part could be seen, on the upper part of the Cross, the face of a man and His body to the waist. On His breast was an equally luminous dove, and nailed to the cross, the body of another man.

A little below the waist, suspended in midair, was to be seen a Chalice and a large Host onto which fell some drops of Blood from the face of the Crucified and from a wound in His breast. These drops ran down over the Host and fell into the Chalice.

Under the right arm of the Cross was Our Lady with her Immaculate Heart in her hand. (It was Our Lady of Fatima with her Immaculate Heart...in her left hand...without a sword or roses, but with a crown of thorns and flames. Under the left arm (of the Cross) some big letters, as it were, of crystal clear water running down over the Altar, formed these words: 'Grace and Mercy.' I understood that it was the mystery of the Most Holy Trinity that was shown to me.

Our prayers and sacrifices by and of themselves avail nothing unto salvation from Hell or unto sanctification. Actually, when prayed with a spirit of sinful pride, such prayers and sacrifices work unto our greater damnation.

An incident in Padre Pio's life brings this out. Someone praised him for his sacrifice as being salutary for many. Our saint perceived the demonic within this apparently pious comment. He then proceeded to chastise the man. Padre Pio's sacrifices by and of themselves were totally *useless.* Only as being sanctified through, *in and into* Christ's Holy Sacrifice does any sacrifice become of eternal worth.

Only *the Sacrifice* avails unto salvation. Only sacrifice through, in and by *the Sacrifice* avail unto salvation and sanctification. Sacrifice is the work of the Blessed Trinity as Tuy emphasizes. Suffering Mary is *the Channel* through whom salutary graces come to those who will comprise the Elect. One *must* accept God's Plan of Salvation or be damned.

The Father, Son and Holy Ghost (the latter under the figure of a luminous dove equal in brightness to the Father) are represented in their perfect distinction. The Mystery of Salvation concerns a double movement of *procession,* of *(katabasis) descent,* and then of *conversion,* going *back up (ana ba sis)* following the great theological theme of *exitus* and *reditus.*(These words are theological terms which would bring us too far afield to treat in any detail). It is the Mystery of Salvation.

CONSECRATION AND REPARATION

Consecration, reparation, prayer and sacrifice form the challenging logon of the God-given message of Fatima from the appearances of the angel in 1916, to the climacteric salutary theophany of 1929. *Consecrate* yourself. Allow the *grace and mercy* of salvation to be applied to you, in belief and in deed, so that you can be made sacred (or *secrated with*) the all Holy God.

As St. Augustine observed: *"God became man so that man could become God."* However, in contradiction to gnosticism, man is not saved in Christ becoming man. Rather, *only the Elect* are saved from eternal Hell, by their becoming like unto Christ--*Christ Crucified!* Redemption is a personal affair. Each must become *like unto Christ-Crucified* through the salutary graces which emanate from *the Holy Sacrifice.*

Notice that the salutary theophany occurred at an altar upon which the Canonized Mass Prayers were said. This was to show forth that which alone attains salvation--*the Holy Sacrifice prayed as instituted by Christ.*

In the salutary theophany, Christ is altar, priest and sacrifice. At each valid Mass, through ordained priests, once again Christ is altar, priest and sacrifice.

Only as our sacrifices are done through, *in and into* the Holy Mass (Sacrifice) are they acceptable to God unto salvation. How can we escape (eternal Hell) if we neglect, despise or reject *so great salvation* (Hb 2:3)--salvation *as Jesus decreed*, salvation through that Holy Mass which led Padre Pio to become like unto Christ-Crucified?

CHAPTER FIVE

THE BLESSED VIRGIN MARY AND PADRE PIO'S MASS

Padre Pio recited many rosaries every day. Hundreds of his *Hail Marys* praised Our Lady daily. The Blessed Virgin and her Rosary are intimately bound up with the Holy Sacrifice of the Mass.

One of God's angels, Gabriel, is chosen to disclose God's Plan to The Blessed Human Person--the Jewish girl, Mariam.

> Hail, Mariam, the full channel of all of God's graces to mankind. You are *the blessed human person--the Blessed Mother* (Lk 1:28, 29). Through you comes *the* blessed human nature of our Saviour. Through you, the Elect are born unto salvation.

Here is the meaning of this angelic greeting. Salvation comes to and through Mariam--the blessed human person. No wonder God is pleased with our *Hail Mary's.* God saves some of us sinners since He primarily loves *the Immaculata*--the only sinless human person. As it were, God's infinite love encountered the boundlessly lovable (because she alone was sinless) human person. As a result, she was not only filled with *all graces,* but became *the channel of all graces.*

> You, Mariam, are *the blessed human person* for your fully believing in God's Revelation (Lk 1:45).

In perfect humility, Mariam responds:

> All people will call me *the blessed human person,* since God gives *the great and only blessing* through me. God gives *The Blessed One,* Jesus Christ and His graces through me (Lk 1:48).

The Source, Sustenance and Summit of any and all blessings given to sinful Hell-destined mankind is the Holy Sacrifice--the Blessing Sacrifice. Here is your only blessing--your only way to escape eternal Hell. Here is *the* Sacrifice which opened up Heaven to the *only Heaven-deserving* human person, Mariam, and thus, to you, if you are numbered among the Elect.

God's Saving Will materialized at the Incarnation. The Second Person of the Triune God assumed a human nature. He became flesh of the Virgin Mary by the power of the Holy Ghost because of the loving mercy of God the Father.

At every valid Mass-consecration, by the power of the Holy Ghost *through Mary,* we could contend that Christ becomes flesh and blood in a more miraculous way than He did at the Incarnation. Mere bread and wine are *transubstantiated* into Christ--Sacrifice and Sacrament. What an awesome miracle of love--a miracle of love which flows from the initial encounter of Infinite Love with the *only* boundless lovable human person, Mary.

MARY AND THE HOLY GHOST

If anyone wishes to know how the bread is changed into the Body of Jesus Christ,

*I will tell him. The Holy Ghost
overshadows the priest and acts on him
as He acted on the Blessed Virgin Mary.*
(St. John Damascene)

In a special way, we are in the age of the Holy
Ghost and of Our Lady. The Mass is
accomplished *in and by the Holy Ghost.* He is *the
Sanctifier.* Each Mass is done (or not done) *only
by a priest. Only a priest* can say or celebrate
Mass. *Only* the *fiat* of a validly functioning priest
can renew or re-do the Marian *fiat* so as to bring
into our midst the Saving Event and the Saving
Person.

Through each properly ordained priest, at each
valid Mass, the Holy Ghost makes present (brings
about) and *accomplishes salvation through
Christ's Person and Sacrifice.* Through the
priest, the Sanctifier comes to abide *in and with
the Holy Sacrament*--the Son of God made flesh,
dwelling among us.

Here, the Holy Ghost, through Mary, continues
to bring about and accomplish salvation through
Christ her Son and His Sacrifice. From the

Incarnation into eternity, where Christ is, there is Mary. Mary is the Co-Redemptrix. Her *"Let it be done unto me as God wills"* was--by God's freely chosen necessity--needed, and is ever needed to bring Jesus into being *in her flesh* in the Holy Sacrifice and Sacrament; and, *in the spirit* of each of the Elect.

Each priest is like unto Mary. As it were, once again decent mankind awaits his response to God's Will. Will he imitate Mary? Will he say and mean *"Let it be done according to Thy Will?"* *"Let this, my Mass, be done by me according to Thy Will."* I will say the Canonized Mass as instituted by Christ. I will be humble like unto Mary. Let Thy Will--not man's--be done!

Each priest is like unto Mary by his *fiat,* now expressed in the Christ-given words of the Offertory and Consecration. However, each priest also acts through (or is *under)* Mary. Why? *The Holy Ghost's prime agent for incarnating Christ is Mary--the channel of all salutary graces.* Jesus, Saviour, comes through Mary. This is a great Marian mystery which was confirmed in our times by St. Maximillian Kolbe. He assures us: Mary, the only sinless human person is related to the Holy Ghost in a most exalted and unique manner.

St. Maximillian Kolbe reminds us that, the human nature of Jesus is to the Second Person of the Triune Godhead as--yet, in a far lesser but similar way--Mary is to the Third Person of the Triune God, the Holy Ghost. As the Son of God assumed the perfect and sinless human nature, so in a similar way did the Holy Ghost *take over* and *work through* the only sinless human person-- Mary. Thus, Mary is *the channel of all graces.*

According to God's freely chosen Providence, God acts salutarily towards us sinners *only* through the sinless human person and through Christ's sinless human nature. According to God's freely chosen Plan, there is no other way to be saved. No wonder the Church has always said: *"De Maria, numquam satis."* One can *never* satisfactorily praise Our Lady. She is the antithesis of Eve. Eve *mothered* sin. Mary *mothers* salvation!

CHAPTER SIX

PADRE PIO'S MASS IS CANONIZED

The Canonized Mass is the Mass Liturgy *dogmatized* by the *sensus et praxis fidelium.* This (the Tridentine Mass Liturgy) is the Mass defined (instituted) by Christ, and forever fixed within the Sacred Deposit of the Catholic Faith; the Mass finalized in Apostolic Tradition; and the Mass dogmatically decreed to be canonical by Pope Saint Pius V. Let's briefly illustrate why we refer to this, the essence of our Catholicism as the Canonized or *binding par* Mass Liturgy.

IRREFUTABLE EVIDENCE

As early as 88 A.D., Pope St. Clement of Rome (Martyr and fourth Pope after St. Peter) wrote in his letter to the Corinthians that *Jesus Christ Himself* defined the Mass--all of the essential parts of the Mass. The Canonized Mass, like the Sacraments, was *instituted by Christ--not by men.*

St. Justin Martyr (in the year 155--in his writings)

stated that *Our Lord Himself,* after His Resurrection, *taught the Apostles exactly how to say Mass.* Dare not anyone reject this *saint's* testimony--the testimony of a saint living only a century after the Church's beginning.

St. Ambrose, in the year 360 (approximately) wrote *De Sacramentis.* In this book, we can find all of the essentials of the Tridentine or Canonized Mass Prayers.

Then, (in the year 450) came the *Leonine Sacramentary* of Pope St. Leo I (also called Leo the Great) and the *Gelasian Sacramentary* of Pope Gelasius I (in 498). In their original forms, these contained the precise Mass Liturgy later defined as *Tridentine.*

The Council of Trent was called in 1545, and lasted a record 18 years, ending in 1563. This Council was *dogmatic, i.e.* infallibly protected by the Holy Ghost, in stark contrast to Vatican Council II, which was pastoral by definition of both Pope John XXIII and of Pope Paul VI, and therefore, *not infallibly protected* by the Holy

Ghost, except where previously defined dogmatic pronouncements were reiterated, which was rare.

The Council of Trent *merely* officially, bindingly, and dogmatically acknowledged the fact that the Canonized Mass Prayers were instituted by Christ Himself! The Council of Trent dogmatically imposed the *Missale Romanum*--the Canonized Mass as instituted by Christ. The Fathers of Trent reverently confirmed that *all of the words of the Canonized Liturgy* have come:

> **out of the very words of the Lord, the traditions of the Apostles, and [regarding unessential words] the pious institutions of holy pontiffs.**
> (Trent, Sess. xxii)

The dogmatic Council of Trent directed Pope Paul IV to issue an Apostolic Constitution on the *Missale Romanum*, but he died shortly after the Council closed (in 1563). It was 7 years after the Council (in 1570) that St. Pius V (who became Pope two years after the Council) issued the Bull *Quo Primum,* ordering the perpetually binding imposition of the Christ-Mass, the Mass instituted by Christ Himself, thereafter known as the Tridentine Mass. *It is this Mass* which is the Canonized Mass. *It is this Mass which made Padre Pio a saint.*

To *canonize* this Mass is to **dogmatize it forever.** To *canonize Mass Prayers* means to sanction, to declare as being the standard, or par, and to make binding, as a living dogma of liturgical (God-directed) morals.

The Sacred Deposit of Faith canonized this Mass. Apostolic Tradition canonized it. The *sensus et praxis* of the faithful from the time of Christ canonized it. It was pronounced to be official and binding by the dogmatic Councils of Florence and, especially, Trent--which Councils (as part of the Extraordinary Magisterium) are of themselves infallible now and always.

Padre Pio prayed only the Canonized Mass Liturgy of the Latin Rite. He prayed this Mass so intensely that he became the most outstanding priest who ever celebrated this liturgy. To understand, appreciate and properly relate to

Padre Pio, one must come to an understanding and love of the Canonized Latin Mass.

THE LATIN MASS

The Mass that made Padre Pio was in Latin. It is not difficult to learn enough Latin to understand and appreciate the Latin used in the Holy Sacrifice of the Mass.

Recent history proves that Latin makes the Canonized Mass into the flawless and perfect gem that it is. One cannot improve a flawless and perfect gem by mutation. One can only destroy it.

History proves that vernacularizing the liturgy always perverted and sacrileged the Mass. These facts should help you to have a positive attitude to the Latin Liturgy of the Latin Rite. This positive attitude will be of tremendous help to you in coming to understand and appreciate more fully the Canonized Mass prayers, which constituted the Mass that made Padre Pio.

Generally speaking, to pray the Holy Mass more fully, it is very helpful to know *Mass Latin*. Let me illustrate with a few examples concerning the *GLORIA*.

BENEDICIMUS TE

Benedicimus te--we speak well of Thee. Why is this not--we BLESS Thee? *Benedicere* ordinarily means *to speak well of. Benedicere*-- only when validly used by God's validly ordained priest, BLESSES AS GOD BLESSES--meaning to *metamorphasize* or to destroy and resurrect (or recreate). Therefore, *only God* and *validly ordained and validly functioning priests* BLESS. All others, at best, can only *speak well of* or *be happy for.*

GRATIAS...TUAM

Gratias agimus tibi propter magnam gloriam tuam. Gratias agimus--we do or live THANKS. We strive to live and to be THANKS TO GOD.

The Latin is precise. Meditate on it.

Propter magnam gloriam tuam--We strive to be A THANKS TO GOD *because of* or motivated by, the goal of reflecting and attesting to God's great glory. God's *glory* will be attained and attested by the souls suffering in Hell forever and ever; as well as, by the ecstatic Elect in eternal Heaven.

Either way, each praises God for His Glory. At the *GLORIA,* I pray that I may reflect and attest to God's great glory--His grace and mercy--for all eternity in Heaven *rather than* reflecting and *actively* attesting to God's justice--also God's glory--for all eternity in Hell.

QUI...NOSTRAM

Qui tollis peccata mundi, suscipe deprecationem nostram--Thou, O God, *tollis*--take from us--our sins. You are our only Prayer--to have sins taken away. You provide the Elect with the *toll* which ransoms them from Hell.

Suscipe deprecationem nostram--Receive our urgent plea (plea--singular, not plural). I have one, and only one, need: to have my sins taken away. *Ferre, tolle, latus sum*--these are the three Latin words that are played on. To carry, to take away, to be handed over--these *English cognates* apply to *ferre, tolle; latus sum.*

Thou, O God, take away sins. I give away myself to Thee in *OB-LATUS* or in *Oblation*, as one *most fully handed over to Thee.* Thou Who takes away (*tollis*) sins, let my being given up to Thee (my *oblatio*) be acceptable to Thee, so that my sins may be *taken away.*

SUSCIPE, SANCTE PATER

Suscipe, sancte Pater--Receive, Heavenly Father--prepares us for and reflects the *suscipe* of the offering of Christ for my sins and then later on, the *suscipe Sancta Trinitas*...and the *suscipiat* response to the Priest's plea that his sacrifice and yours may be acceptable to God the Father. You can begin to see how Padre Pio understood the

Latin Mass Liturgy. You can see how knowing Latin will help you to understand and appreciate the Mass prayers. On a primer lever, you'll notice as I did, that certain Latin prepositions are irreplaceable.

For example, we give God thanks *propter* His glory: *propter*--because of, on account of, as rational creatures most thankful for. Listen to and think with the Church in its language so that you can pray with the Church in that Mass which was CANONIZED IN ITS *LATIN* FORM.

As Padre Pio said the Mass, as it were, he *focused on* certain Latin words. As with Padre Pio, so also will it be with you. As you pray the Mass again and again, key words will become highlighted in your mind and heart. These words will take on ever more meaning until--if God graces you, and you so live as to be graced--the Mass prayers will take on the same deep and unfathomable meaning as they did for Padre Pio, the one and only stigmatist-priest of the Canonized Mass.

MODERN POPES MANDATE LATIN

Vatican II prescribed that Latin be retained, especially as it exists in the Canonized Latin Liturgy. Pope John XXIII most solemnly decreed that the Church *must retain this language which is "universal, immutable and non-vernacular."* Pope John concluded his most solemn and binding Apostolic Constitution with these words:

> We now in the full consciousness of Our Office and in virtue of Our Authority, decree and command: Bishops and superiors general of religious orders... shall be on their guard lest anyone under their jurisdiction...writes against the use of Latin, either in the teaching of the higher sacred studies or in the Liturgy or...makes light of the Holy See's will in this regard or interprets it falsely.
> (The Apostolic Constitution, Veterum Sapientia, Pope John XXIII, February 22, 1962)

Concerning this Apostolic Constitution, Father Raymond Miller, C.SS.R., reported from Rome:

> Few, if any, Papal documents in all

history have been signed by a Pope with more striking emphasis on his authority and determination. He did the signing... in St. Peter's Basilica...on the Feast of the Chair of St. Peter...surrounded by all the Cardinals resident in Rome.

(The Priest, July 1962)

Finally, we cite Pope Paul VI:

When the integrity of faith has been preserved, it is necessary also to safeguard its proper mode of expression, lest, by the careless use of words, we occasion, God forbid, the rise of false opinions regarding the most sublime of mysteries...These [Mass] formulas are adapted to men of all times and of all places...The Church, therefore, with the long labor of centuries and the help of the Holy Ghost, has established a canon or rule of language confirming it with the authority of the Councils. This canon or rule must be religiously preserved. Let no one presume to change it at his own pleasure or under the pretext of new science...Given at

43

Rome, at St. Peter's, the third day of
September, the Feast of Pope Saint Pius
X, in the year 1965, the third year of our
Pontificate.
(Encyclical, Mysterium Fidei, On Eucharistic Doctrine and
Worship, Pope Paul VI, Sept. 3, 1965)

Latin--not because it is *not* the vernacular, but
Latin, as eternally fixed in the significant words
of the Canonized Liturgy--is the official and
solemnly mandated language of the Church. The
Canonized Mass of our rite is to be kept in its
defined or canonical *Latin form.* So have
councils and popes bindingly decreed for all times
and for all places. So decrees the *sensus et praxis
fidelium.*

Therefore, *this* and this alone should be the Mass
for Roman Catholics of the Latin Rite. Such is
God's Will as specified by popes; pope-approved
dogmatic councils; the *sensus et praxis fidelium;*
Apostolic Tradition; and ultimately, Christ
Himself.

CHAPTER SEVEN

PADRE PIO'S INSIGHTS ON PRAYER

The prayer objectively considered is *the Holy Sacrifice*--willed by God from eternity past; realized and actualized on Good Friday (in the first Mass and in the Bloody Sacrifice of Calvary); re-presented (and thus realized) at every Canonized Mass; and realized so as to constitute, as well as to *goal* eternal Heaven. (Apoc 5:6, 11-14).

The Sacrifice applied constitutes Heaven. That's why the Limbo of the Just (*Hell* in the creed) could only be emptied *after the Sacrifice: "He (Christ) descended into Hell."*

To and from *the prayer of the Holy Sacrifice* flowed Padre Pio's life of prayer and all of his sayings on prayer. To be sure, if any of these sayings are (or seem to be) incompatible with this truth, such a saying must be rejected. All of us should be convinced that Padre Pio did not pray and could not have prayed with a heretical mindset. He prayed from, in and into the

Canonized Mass. The only stigmatist-priest who ever lived could not have prayed or celebrated anything but the Canonized Mass. He could not have done so and remained the stigmatist-priest.

Only the Canonized Mass is totally compatible with that which made Padre Pio be who he was in time and is eternally. The Canonized Mass was manifested in Padre Pio to such a degree that he received the stigmata. He lived as Christ, suffering His Passion during his Masses, as well as (to a lesser extent) between Masses.

It was the Canonized Mass which defined Padre Pio. That's obvious to anyone who knows Padre Pio and the Holy Sacrifice of the Mass. Let us consider a small sampling of his comments on prayer--always in the light of that Mass which defined Padre Pio.

"Prayer is the effusion of our hearts into God's." Classically stated, prayer is *the lifting of one's mind and heart to God.* Does this latter definition seem to be man-centered, sterile, uninviting and even incomplete? God's *Heart* towards us is *His Saving Will.* Only through the Holy Sacrifice can one become *infused.* Only thus can one's heart be *effused into God's Heart.*

"One searches for God in books; one finds Him in meditation." Meditation reflects and flows from *the Holy Sacrifice of the Mass*--especially, as expressed in the Priest's prayers within the Canonized Mass. You will *find God in the Holy Sacrifice of the Mass*--God's *"so great salvation (Hb 2:3)."* You will find God not because you read, but because you meditate and pray the Mass--the Mass of Padre Pio. Indeed, one finds God in meditation on the Canonized Mass. Thus was I blessed.

Sometime after converting to saying the Canonized Mass, I would become awake in the early morning hour of four o'clock, with Mass prayers floating in my mind. I meditated on these prayers. The fruit of these imperfect and wanting meditations is my translation of the Canonized Mass--MY BASIC MISSAL. (available from MAETA)

"Be assiduous in your prayers and

meditations." Keep at it! It took me time, effort and God's special graces to unlock and assimilate (although poorly), some of the meanings within the priest-prayers of the one and only Canonized Mass. Don't give up. Be assiduous--until the penny drops. Continually pray and meditate on your God-given (and made into your own) fiducial insights all day long. Let them form the foundation of your praying, suffering and work-- the foundation of your life outside of Mass.

"Prayer must be insistent. Insistence denotes faith." If you salutarily believe, if you have the faith, you will be insistent in your prayers. You will insist on being a beneficiary of the prayer--of being saved from eternal Hell. You will *pray always* (1 Th 5:17)." However, insistent prayer is possible only if your prayer is the Mass. Any other alleged insistent prayer is a sick or worldly obsession--emanating from a twisted psycho-spiritual nature or from Satan, the Deceiver, who is at work today as never before.

Only the Mass can be the source, sustenance and summit of truly insistent prayer. For example, as will be pointed out, the Canonized Mass prays that the living be saved from Hell and be preserved from those things which impede salvation. That's it, nothing else matters! Only this can be authentically insisted upon. What would it profit one if all of the banal offertory petitions within the usual modern liturgy were granted? What does it profit one to gain the whole world and then to suffer in eternal Hell?

When you are praying in God's Presence, examine yourself honestly, speak to Him if you can; if you can't, stay there; let Him *work on you* and don't do anything.

What an apt description of how you should attend Mass (or celebrate Mass, if you are a priest). You're in God's Presence. You are before the tabernacle within which Christ dwells. You are at *the Saving-Deed, re-done before you.*

"The best comfort comes from prayer." For Padre Pio and for us, the only and best prayer is the Mass. As such, it is the best comfort. Examine yourself honestly. See who you are essentially--a sinner who needs the Mass to avoid Hell and to enter Heaven. Pray as you are--a sinner who needs the Mass to avoid Hell. The more you are convinced of this, your essential need, the more you will seek and appreciate the only fulfillment of your only need--the Holy Sacrifice of the Mass.

> Most Holy Trinity, we offer Christ, the Christ Who was born from *the Sacrifice* in reparation for sinners. (the Angelic Prayer of Fatima, 1916)

"Save souls by continuous prayer." Fatima's sentiments are Padre Pio's sentiments. Fatima reminds us that souls can be saved only through Christ.

However, God has give us the Colossians' Mystery (Col 1:24). Somehow, I can make up in my body for what is lacking of the sufferings of Christ in His Body, for the sake of His Body, the Church. This is the Colossians' Mystery.

One among hundreds of thousands of examples of this conviction (being operative in Padre Pio's life) was the example of the Italian lady who cooked Padre Pio's favorite pasta. He graciously thanked her for her thoughtfulness, but refused to eat the pasta--pointing out to her that if he did, two souls wouldn't make it to Purgatory.

Pray the Mass. Save souls. Pray the Mass in all you say and do. Pray the Mass in your prayers, sufferings and daily chores. Imitate Padre Pio. Pray for sinners through the continuous prayer of the Holy Sacrifice of the Mass.

> **I want to be only a poor friar who prays...Far from considering myself better than others, I believe instead that of all those on earth, I am the one who serves the Lord least. By means of this grace, He has given me such a clear view that I see myself obliged more than anyone else to love my Creator.** (7-7-13)

God resists the proud. Are you humble? Do you join Padre Pio in confessing that you are a poor sinner--totally needful of the Holy Sacrifice and the Holy Sacrament?

O my Jesus, forgive us our sins, save us from the fires of Hell--especially those who confess great need of Thy salvation.(the Rosary prayer from Fatima)

With Padre Pio, do you confess that you, more than others, must love God? Do you confess that you are not better than others but that you have obeyed and served God the least?

"The more Our Lady was filled with Heavenly gifts, the more she humbled herself." A sure sign that one is a spiritual fake and hypocrite is that one refuses to humble himself. One refuses to confess that his only need is Salvation. One refuses to pray the Christ-given Holy Sacrifice as the fulfillment of his only need.

Humble yourself. Admit, and live in the conviction, that you are a wretched sinner. As such, your only hope for salvation from eternal Hell is in the Saving-Deed and the Saving-Person--the Holy Sacrifice of the Mass and the Holy Sacrament.

Always embrace the holy Cross of Jesus...Let us climb Calvary without ever tiring, carrying the Cross...Take up then your salvation on the Cross; stretch yourself out on it. Go ahead, and ask the Lord to make you participate in His sufferings and inebriate you with His Cross...to the extent which pleases Him (III).

The more you properly pray the Mass, the more you will become one of Padre Pio's children. The Mass which St. Paul described as *so great salvation* (Hb 2:3) is just that for you and for all other Catholics who pray and live the Canonized Mass. However, to properly and profitably pray this Mass, you must know what is being prayed. By God's providence, such knowledge is available to you and others through reading a proper translation of the Mass (as in MY BASIC MISSAL) and by prayerfully reading and assimilating books such as this one. Then you will be able to join others in praying and living the Mass unto your salvation from Hell unto Heaven.

Keep in mind that you and I--gifted or studied--at best, attain a kindergarten level of understanding, appreciation and love of the Canonized Mass, while Padre Pio, by God's grace and his own graced cooperation, went to the post-graduate level. Certainly, we both have the means--grace and nature upon which grace builds--to attain to the level of a Padre Pio. God is not wanting. It's not God's fault that we aren't holy or holier. It's our own fault. Besides blocking ourselves by not striving, some of us manage to block out the real Padre Pio from our consciousness. How is this accomplished?

Some deny the Source, Sustenance and Summit of his identity. Some, even highly placed enthusiasts, claim that praying, or even saying the Canonized Mass was incidental or accidental to Padre Pio. Such as these know neither Padre Pio, nor the Mass. They should remain silent. They should not malign God by maligning the unique person of Padre Pio. One can't claim devotion to Padre Pio without being entirely devoted to the Mass. Such is absolutely true.

Padre Pio's greatest work is yet to be accomplished. Through his heavenly intercession, the Canonized Mass will be restored to its Christ-given proper place, as taught by the Church throughout the centuries. Writing in Quo Primum, Pope Saint Pius V stated:

> Specifically, do we warn all persons in authority of whatever dignity or rank, and command them *as a matter of strict obedience* never to use or *permit* any ceremonies of Mass prayers *other than the ones contained in this Missal...At no time*...can a priest...ever be forced to use any other way of saying Mass. And...to preclude any scruples of conscience and fear of ecclesial penalties and censures, we declare herewith...by virtue of our Apostolic authority...that this present order and decree...is to last *in perpetuity*...and if...anyone...dare attempt...action contrary to this order... let him know that he has incurred the wrath of Almighty God, and of the Blessed Apostles Peter and Paul. (Italics mine)

Given the history of the Catholic Church, and the decree issued by Pope Saint Pius V, to say nothing of the fact that the modern liturgy is considered a celebration meal and *not a sacrifice*, it is impossible to conceive that Padre Pio, a priest of such holy repute as to receive the stigmata, could ever pray any Mass other than the Canonized Holy Sacrifice of the Mass. Considering the binding, dogmatic decree issued by the pope-saint from whom Padre Pio took his religious name, it simply would not compute!

CHAPTER EIGHT

THE MASS-MADE MYSTIC STIGMATIST

Far from considering myself better than others, I believe instead that of all those on earth, I am the one who serves the Lord least. By means of this grace he has given me such a clear view that I see myself obliged more than anyone else to love my Creator (7-7-1913).

Beginning with his early life, Padre Pio was led to the abiding conviction of himself as being a *most wretched and vile sinner*, both in potency and in deed. Upon this basis--an *experienced need*--was built his flaming love of Christ as the only One who could, did, and would fulfill him.

As we have seen, Padre Pio was fully convinced of the basic Catholic Mass-related convictions. A mystic is a *fully alive Catholic*. Very few in our day live, even minimally, as Catholics. To come to deeply understand and appreciate this mystic, you must go beyond the ordinarily miraculous--

his bi-locations, gifts of seeing souls, gifts of understanding foreign languages, etc. Go straight to the heart of Padre Pio. The heart of Padre Pio was the Holy Mass. All else is superficial or non-essential. God's greatest gift among us--the Holy Sacrifice of the Mass--enabled Padre Pio to be the first and greatest mystic-stigmatist-priest.

THE MYSTIC OF THE CANONIZED MASS

Because he was so visible and active, we tend not to think of Padre Pio as a mystic. However, he was one of the greatest mystics produced by the Catholic Church. He was directly produced by the very essence of the Catholic Church, the Canonized Mass. He was this Mass personified. He is one of the best fruits of the Canonized Mass--the heart of Christ's Church.

Every informed and honest intellectual knows that the Canonized Mass is the heart of Christ's Church. Even Martin Luther knew this: *tolle missam, tolle ecclesiam--take away the Mass, take away the Church.*

Indeed, the Canonized Mass is the Church. Without the Canonized Mass, one no longer has the Latin Rite of the Catholic Church, as living history is now proving and, as a properly and plenarily pope-ing pope, at some future time, will dogmatically decree, in order to remedy the ever-growing disunity and corruption within the existential church.

Essentially, the Canonized Mass is the *re-doing of Calvary* and the *re-coming of Christ*, in as much as both are possible by the power of Almighty God, into our here and now. Padre Pio, in praying the Holy Mass, not only re-presented Calvary, but also *re-presented the Crucified Christ*. In the past, mystics have faded in and out of living the core of the Salutary Deed, the Passion of Christ. In Padre Pio, God gave us the final fruit, the best of fruits of the Canonized Mass Liturgy.

MYSTICAL MOMENTS OF PARTICIPATION

Daily, our priest-mystic participated in the

Passion, in preparation for his next Mass and as a continuing effect of his last Mass. Generally at Mass, the Offertory, the Consecration and Holy Communion constituted key mystical moments for Padre Pio. In preparing for his next Mass, and in living within the afterglow and effects of his last Mass, Padre Pio's thoughts would be:

Think (of) and meditate on the Victim, Who offers Himself to Divine Justice, absorbing the price of your redemption.

Psycho-spiritually, Padre Pio became the great mystic that he was because he, more than most others, realized his and our need for salvation from Hell and salvation into Heaven. He appreciated Christ--Victim, our only Redeemer from Hell. The more one realizes the need, the more one appreciates the solution or answer to this need. It's that simple. It's that profound.

Out of Padre Pio's intensely experienced need, came his outstanding embrace of the answer--Christ-Crucified, or the Holy Sacrifice of the Mass. When he wasn't saying, in prayer and by participation, the Canonized Mass, our mystic priest was praying and living the Mass. Outside of Mass, he lived in the afterglow of his last Mass; and, as a preparation for his next Mass. His final preparation was for the never ending Heavenly Mass, *the Lamb once slain* adored eternally (Apoc 5:12-14).

During the day and at night, the entire Passion of Christ was relived by (or in) the exalted mystic-stigmatist-priest. Padre Pio gave himself up--body and soul--to Christ-Crucified. He loved and lived Christ-Crucified every conscious moment of his life. At night, he continued to suffer. He suffered the agony, the trial, the climb to Calvary, and to a lesser extent than he did at Mass, the Sacrifice of Calvary. Our saint lived *the Holy Sacrifice--* that *passion and cross*, which, at the recitation of each *Angelus,* we confess to be our only salvation.

Without the Holy Sacrifice of the Canonized Mass, Padre Pio wouldn't have been and couldn't have been the mystic-stigmatist-priest that he became. Padre Pio loved the Canonized Mass so much that, had he been allowed to do so, he would have celebrated this Mass every moment of his life.

THE MASS--CALVARY

Suffering the entire Passion and, especially, the sufferings of Calvary, was reserved for Padre Pio at each of his Masses. Here, as few if any, priests before him, he prayed and lived the Mass, the Passion and dying of Christ. At each of his Masses, this unique priest suffered (as much as humanly possible), the Passion of Christ. Somehow, he became one wound from head to toe, inwardly and outwardly. Was he not the greatest mystic that ever lived? Did he not unite with Christ in *His* Mass, as no priest has ever done?

At each Mass, he suffered Calvary. He suffered the crowning with thorns. He suffered all else that Christ suffered. He lived, not him, but Christ-Crucified in him. The miracles of Padre Pio's life testify to this. Padre Pio's stigmata, which were visible to men of the twentieth century, testify to this.

As many have officially testified, the wounds on his hands were so deep, that they went through his hands. We cannot doubt. We dare not doubt. He lived as each of us is challenged to live. He lived the Mass. He lived, not him, but Christ-Crucified.

There, but for me--there, but for my lack of love--go I. At least, let me praise Christ as realized in this person. Thus, may I become one of Padre Pio's children. Thus, will I obtain his special protection and help.

PARTICIPANT IN THE PASSION

Christ-Suffering or Christ-Oblated lives in each one who properly prays and lives the Canonized Mass. Whenever Christ lives in one who properly prays and lives the Canonized Mass; or whenever Christ lives in any soul this side of death, He does so to be oblated in (or into) that person. He does so to suffer and to die.

Padre Pio said, prayed and lived the Canonized Mass Liturgy. This Mass incorporated him into Christ, defining him into being forever who he is. In a manner awesome to behold, Christ-Oblated, Christ-Suffering, *materialized* in Padre Pio as in few others before him. Through, with and in Christ, he was oblated as he prayed Mass prayers such as: *Suscipe, Sancte Pater hanc Immaculatum Hostiam.* Christ, as offered, was actively reflected, and materialized in this mystic priest, who suffered the Stigmata (as well as--with St. Teresa, the rare mystic gift of transverberation).

Padre Pio offered himself through, with and in Christ. The Colossians' Mystery was realized in him:

> *I make up what is lacking in the [desired] sufferings of Christ, in my body for the sake of His Body, the Church.* (Col 1:24, as the original Greek states)

In an exemplary way, Padre Pio agreed to make up in his own body [by and through the Mass] what was lacking in the suffering of Christ [as desired] to be accomplished in Padre Pio's body for the sake of Christ's Mystical Body, the Church.

CONSECRATED

Padre Pio's offering was especially consummated in the Consecration prayers of the Mass. As it were, when Padre Pio, as Christ-priest, redid the Saving Will, as Christ instituted, Christ redid His salutary Will in Padre Pio.

As this "Christ-priest," blessed, he was annihilated and metamorphasized by Christ. He became Christ to the degree that he became the stigmatist-priest. Padre Pio gave his body: *"This, my body, O Lord, is given to Thee to be like unto Thy body."* Christ honored this humble priest's desires. Christ united Padre Pio's body to His Body, to be in a like manner broken--through, in and with Christ's Body--to be taken into the Colossians' Mystery (Col 1:24) and so to be broken, that like Christ, his life-blood would be shed for sinners.

Padre Pio's life was one of joyful Christ-suffering or Christ being oblated in and through him. It was his joy, his very life, to suffer for the sake of building up Christ's Body, the Church. He strove to complete what is lacking of Christ's [desired] sufferings in his own body for the sake of Christ's body, the Church (Col 1:24).

SIMILI MODO

At the Consecration of the wine--the wine is annihilated and is transubstantiated into Christ's Blood. Padre Pio's blood or his natural ambitions were annihilated from living for (or from) his flesh and the world. He died to the flesh and to the world. He died in order to live--not him, but Christ, Christ-Suffering, in him. His life-force or his ambitions were transubstantiated. Not only were they metamorphasized so that he could know what was the perfect Will of God for him (Rms 12:2); but, he was empowered, or graced, to live that perfect Will--Christ-Crucified through and in Padre Pio (Ga 2:20).

IN MEMORIAM CHRISTI

In saying the Canonized Mass, Padre Pio, as it were, had his own body broken and his own blood shed, in order to be metamorphasized by Christ into Christ's life-force flowing into and through Padre Pio, so as to define him into being who he is for eternity--*in memoriam Christi*--one taken into the Memory, Christ.

Padre Pio lived the Canonized Mass, especially the Consecration: he gave all of his blood. When he died, his veins were found to be emptied of blood. All of what God gave to him was given to Christ-Suffering. As Padre Pio offered Christ the Victim, he, too, was offered in Christ to God the Father, as oblated in and through Christ-Sacrificed. As Padre Pio consecrated--annihilated bread and wine--he was annihilated. As Padre Pio, Christ-priest, consecrated--created Christ-Suffering and Dying for our sins--he himself was transformed into a suffering and dying *alter Christus*.

Only the Canonized Mass could have made or

created Padre Pio. It fueled his ability to live his life *in memoriam*--into the memory of Christ-Suffering or Christ-Sacrificed. Remember, Padre Pio received the stigmata, only after saying the Canonized Mass--one month after ordination, first in a hidden way and then, continually visible for fifty years, until his death. Essentially, Padre Pio was the special product of the Canonized Mass.

THE SAINT OF THE CANONIZED MASS

I recall a verbal encounter that I had recently with a top-ranking Padre Pio promoter and enthusiast. She told me that several influential priests whom she consulted rejected the image of Padre Pio as being devoted to the *Holy Sacrifice*. They believed only in a holy meal, just as heretics believe. Therefore, she politely warned me not to associate Padre Pio with the Canonized Holy Sacrifice of the Mass.

Let the truth prevail. Padre Pio was the only stigmatist-priest in the history of the Church. His Mass was the Canonized Latin Liturgy. Christ's

Canonized Mass made him *who he was* and *who he is* for all eternity. Such is the inspiration and efficacy of the Holy Sacrifice of the Mass. Let the saintly example of the Saint of the Canonized Mass inspire you to attend, exalt and promulgate that Mass which made him to be who he is.

CHALLENGE

Some try to divorce Padre Pio from the Mass that defined him to be who he was and is. Still others make our saint just like the rest of us--the only difference being that he had certain sensational charisma. Some even dare to portray Padre Pio as a sickly and weak man always on the verge of natural collapse. At the beginning of my investigation, after reading several books on our saint, I, too, was in danger of developing a false notion of him. Then, I read Oscar De Liso's <u>Padre Pio The Priest Who Bears The Wounds of Christ</u>. (McGraw-Hill, 1960) Many of my questions and doubts were resolved.

Padre Pio wasn't a sickly lad. He was a boy and

young man, who suffered intensely out of love for Christ and to save souls. As a result of this, periodically, his strong body would wear down, or even break down.

Padre Pio didn't live in luxury. In fact, he lived in saintly poverty. The furnishings in his room were like those of the Cure' of Ars, St. John Vianney. Like other exalted mystics, his regular diet was about four ounces of food.

Padre Pio didn't love "the poor," those who shirked God-given individual responsibility. He loved Christ exclusively and totally--with all his mind, heart and soul. From that love, he related to others--always, and in all ways possible, for the salvation of their immortal souls.

In his youth, Padre Pio was characterized by his anti-social behavior. He played, or rather prayed, alone. Typically, he would make a cross and meditate on Christ's crucifixion for hours.

Padre Pio wasn't dumb. He was very intelligent. He excelled in the seminary in spite of (as well as on account of) his prolonged fastings and many hours of prayer and meditation. In his letters, he frequently quoted the saints.

Padre Pio studied and learned the Liturgy of the Canonized Mass as very few before him ever did and as very few after him ever will. What is presented in this book about the Canonized Mass doesn't come close to what Padre Pio knew about this liturgy. One can only come to a better appreciation of Padre Pio through a better knowledge and more conscious and deeper praying of the Canonized Mass.

Note that the holy environment that surrounded Padre Pio didn't hinder him from becoming who he was and is. While it is true that many complained to his superior about his three hour Masses, and some complained about his strictness in the confessional, yet, on the whole, the psycho-spiritual milieu of his time, supported and did not stifle this mystic stigmatist priest.

We will have to wait a long time before our psycho-spiritual milieu will support and encourage any priest who behaves like Padre Pio. Very few, especially priests and bishops, would tolerate such a stigmatist priest. For example, few (if any) bishops would tolerate Padre Pio in his three hour Masses.

Therefore, know and appreciate the Canonized Mass, which defined Padre Pio to be who he was in life and is now in eternity. To be one of Padre Pio's spiritual children, is to know, love and live the Canonized Mass that made Padre Pio.

CHAPTER NINE

PADRE PIO & THE ALTAR OF SACRIFICE

Padre Pio said his Mass at an altar, never at a table; except at his last Mass, when he was wheeled in to face the people. At this last Mass, in obedience to "ecclesiastical authority," he was humiliated with Christ.

As Christ exposed before the gaze of the crowd at Calvary suffered, so was Padre Pio forced to *suffer his last Mass before the gaze of the crowd.* This was his final humiliation with Christ-Crucified. How he must have suffered! Like Christ, he suffered as one obedient to God's Will. How humbling was Padre Pio's last Mass.

With Christ, he seemed to be abandoned, as the altar of sacrifice was replaced by a table. God is to be worshipped at the altar, not at a table. This was always true. This will always be true--an *altar, never a table.* Padre Pio's life was one of *sacrifice, not of banqueting.*

As dissenting heretics displace the altar with a

73

table, they insult God. In Heaven, *Christ the Sacrifice* and *Christ the Altar*--never a table-- predominate; as God's Bible assures us (especially in the Apocalypse); as St. Augustine confirms. God is fixated on the altar. From the beginning of His revelations to us until their climax, the altar predominates.

Wherever any pre-figurement of Christ's Sacrifice was made by man and accepted by God--there was an altar--never, a table. Where such sacrifices were once prescribed by God, there existed the altar and the Temple of God's Old Dispensation--the altar and Temple of Jerusalem.

Where Christ's Sacrifice exists--***there are both altar and church-temple.*** Calvary wasn't a place to eat, drink and be merry. Calvary was the site of the Bloody Sacrifice, not of the happy meal. There was no table at Calvary. So also, the Unbloody Sacrifice of Calvary can never fittingly occur at such a table. Likewise, each valid Mass is the Holy Sacrifice, not a happy meal.

Where God had slain the first animal in sacrifice,

there was the first pre-figurement of the altar. God clothed Adam and Eve with animal skins-- the fruits of His animal sacrifice.

God demanded animal sacrifices on altars of stone--to pre-figure the Holy Sacrifice on Mount Calvary. Humble Abel complied. Proud Cain rejected God's liturgical Will. Cain offered to God *as Cain decided to offer*. God rejected Cain and his plan of salvation. Today, the *Cains among us* insist that they come to God and God comes to them at a *table for a meal* and not God's way-- through an Altar for Sacrifice.

Why did God command His people: *Build my altar not from your works--out of hewn stone--but of natural stone* (Lev 6)?

The Christ-altar was Christ's Body, upon which His Blood was shed. Christ's Body was *natural-- not* artificial or contrived by men.

CHRIST THE ALTAR

"The blood of sacrifice is to be poured round the foot of the altar (Lev 1:6)." *Blood poured* defined God's altar. Wherever blood is shed in accord with God's salutary prescriptions--there is an altar.

Ultimately and in reality, the Blood was poured on Christ's Body. Thus, Christ's Body is the altar (as St. Gregory Nazianzen states). Here is the altar which Christ takes with Him into Eternity: "My Body broken and given to the Elect now and forever." Christ's Body had to be broken so that His Blood be shed upon it--on behalf of His Elect ones.

St. Augustine called Christ the altar--both of Calvary and of Heaven. Somehow, that altar, the Body of Christ, is also the Elect. That's why every Catholic altar has an altar stone. Altar stones contain the relics of martyrs-- representatives of the Body of Christ.

Christ is the whole of His Sacrifice--Priest,

Sacrifice and Altar (Heb 13). The early Fathers of the Church frequently give the name *Altar* to the celestial Christ. Ignatius, for example, speaking of the Son returned to the Father, speaks of Christ as *Altar and Temple.*

> *Hasten to come to the one temple of God, as to the one Altar, to the one Jesus Christ* (Magnes., 7,2F.P.1, 236).

The Apocalypse discloses that Christ, the living Altar, is before the throne of God (6:9; 8:3-5; 9:13; 11:1; 14:18; 16:7). This defines *the Temple* (11:1; 19; 14:17, 18; 15:5-8; 16:17). *"God is a jealous God* (Na 1:2). *He is very jealous of His Altar and His Church-Temple* (2 Ec 1:14).

God's Bible is clear that His Sacrifice requires an Altar. So, too, the Mass that made Padre Pio requires an Altar. Padre Pio said Mass at the altar except for the time of his *ultimate disgrace.* Perhaps, God provided this "ultimate disgrace" to have Padre Pio more like unto Christ-Crucified-- Christ Crucified exposed to the curious, mocking gaze of the crowd at the Crucifixion.

If we had faith, we should see the heavenly host gathered around the Altar during the Mass. Undoubtedly, the whole heavenly court is then present. (Council of Oxford, 1222)

FOR GOD, THE PEOPLE AND HIMSELF

Obsessed with signs and symbols, this generation neglects, disdains and rejects the essential sign of the God-ordained Priest's position at the Canonized Mass. The Priest is ordained *for himself, for the people and for God.* Here at the Holy Sacrifice, the Priest shows forth and accomplishes all three of these purposes by his positions, actions and words. Destroy these and other signs and symbols, and one destroys the priesthood, as instituted by Christ.

FOR THE PEOPLE

The Priest represents the people to God. He stands for the people. He stands as leader of the people. Therefore, quite logically, he stands in front of the people as the sign of being their *leader*.

Also, as is usual, the Priest stands as the leader of the people *before Christ the Eucharist* to pray for them to God, Who is Christ the Eucharist. The Priest is *pontifex*--the bridge between his people and God. He and he alone stands apart from the people, in front of the people and before God, before the Tabernacle. Most fittingly, the Priest faces the Tabernacle to pray on our behalf to God. So did Padre Pio say every Mass--except, of course, for his last Mass.

FOR GOD

The Priest is ordained to be Christ or God to us. When turned to us, he takes God's place to instruct and to feed. He is God's designated pastor--to instruct, to feed, to heal and to guard His flock. The Priest is Christ, the good shepherd to His flock. He is the father of His children--to instruct them, to warn them, to guide them, to forgive them, to *divinize* them, to exhort them, to scold them, to feed them. By God's infinite love, the Priest is ordained to say Mass. Here, the Priest, as Christ, re-presents the Holy Sacrifice of Calvary and gives Christ, Holy Eucharist.

How is each Priest ordained for himself? As God has enacted His dispensation in the Canonized Mass and its rituals, the Priest and the Priest alone *ministers spiritually as Christ* to the people; and the Priest, and the Priest alone, represents the people in praying to God for their need of salvation and in making that answer present in the Holy Sacrifice out of which comes the Holy Eucharist.

Such a spiritual ministry can be exercised with or without a congregation. Therefore, we can say that each Priest is ordained *for himself.* He is ordained and consecrated to celebrate Mass for the living and the dead, with or without a congregation in attendance. Each Priest is ordained to be a saint. *"Know what you are doing [the Holy Sacrifice] and imitate Him Whom you handle. "*(The bishop's prayer at Padre Pio's ordination)

PADRE PIO MODEL FOR PRIESTS

Each priest, until 1969, was specifically ordained *to offer Sacrifice to God, to celebrate Mass.* Therefore, each priest, up to 1969, was admonished as was Padre Pio:

> **Agnosce quod agis, imitare quod tractas, quatenus, mortis et resurrectionis Domini mysterium celebrans, membra tua a vitiis omnibus et in novitate vitae ambulare studeas.**

> **Come to really know what you have been ordained to do. Be like unto the Sacrifice which you do for yourself and others.Be like unto the Sacrament Whom you bring into existence and as pastor give to your flock.**

> **As you celebrate or bring into being the Sacred Salutary Mysteries--the Saving Deed, the Passion, Death and Resurrection of Christ--die to natural desires within you, desires to live for**

and from your Flesh and other humans. Instead, strive to live in newness of life--that life which is demanded of one who should live, not himself, but Christ-Crucified in him.

The Priest, worthy or unworthy, is God's special instrument. He is challenged to be as he is used-- *in persona Christi*. He is challenged to be--in all of his life--another Christ.

However, St. John Chrysostom assured us that many bishops go to Hell and that a lesser number of priests go to Hell. Being God's instrument-- even saying Mass--doesn't assure anyone that he prays and lives the Mass unto his own salvation from Hell and into eternal glorification through Christ. Being a Christ-priest offers the greatest challenge--to imitate and to become one with Him, Whom one makes present in Sacrifice and handles as Sacrament.

TWO CONFESSIONS ONE ABSOLUTION

God resists the proud and gives His grace to the humble. The more the graces and favours of Jesus grow in your soul, the more you should humble yourself, always keeping in mind the humility of our heavenly Mother, who, the instant she became the Mother of God, declared herself the handmaid of this self-same God...What distresses me the most is that I repay Jesus' love with so much ingratitude. (Padre Pio)

The Priest doesn't confess with the laity. He isn't a layman. He is Christ's priest. However, he too sins. Therefore, he confesses his sins. Likewise, laymen sin. They confess their sins separately.

Confiteor Deo--notice that both (laity and priest) primarily confess to God and not to each other. Sin is an offense against God--as any minimally informed Catholic knows. Priest and laity have offended God. That's why they both seek pardon from God--*not from men, either individually or communally.*

In these non-confessional petitions, we are also reminded of the *essential difference* between priests and laymen. In confession, laymen have the Priest (Christ among us) to impart God's absolution. Laymen are useless and impotent to absolve the Priest or any other human being of sins.

Priests ordained for the Canonized Liturgy were *explicitly ordained to forgive sins.* Before ordination, they were not different from laymen. After ordination, they become Christ among us-- *to forgive and pardon sins or not to do so--* through the Sacrament of Penance. (After 1969, this ordination "gift" is no longer explicitly bestowed.

Remember Padre Pio. He was very harsh and embarrassingly frank *in the confessional.* He came down hard on those who had lost awareness of the horror of sin, so that they once more became conscious of the seriousness of their sins in the Sacrament of Penance.

THE PRIEST ASCENDS TO THE ALTAR

"Jesus, make me an altar for your cross."
(Padre Pio)

Padre Pio's passage from the sacristy to the sanctuary seemed to have been the journey of a man carrying a cross. The brief passage from the sacristy into the sanctuary brings the Priest into a new dimension. Priest and people are separated even more, for now the Priest, *the sacrificer*, is about to leave the lower sanctuary, the place proper to him as a man, in order to ascend unto the altar, where he will act as *Priest*, or *in persona Christi.*

> P. *Introibo ad altar Dei.*
> **I will go unto the altar of God.**
> S. *Ad Deum qui laetificat juventutem meam.*
> **To God, who giveth joy to my youth.**

Before he separates himself even further from the people (so as to enter unto the altar of God) he blesses them: *The Lord be with you,* adding immediately: *Oremus. Let us pray! Let us be united ...in prayer.* The Priest prays twice for himself. He dares to ascend to the Altar of God. He prays with the editorial *we,* as he represents and leads the people. He prays with the humiliating *I,* as he remains himself.

> *Take away from us our iniquities, O Lord, WE beseech Thee, that WE may enter with pure minds into the Holy of Holies.*

> *O Lord, by the merits of Thy saints whose relics lie here, and of all the Saints: deign in Thy mercy to pardon me all MY sins. Amen.*

In this prayer (*Aufer a nobis*) the Priest prays again for spiritual purity for himself. This is your opportunity to join in prayer for the Priest and for yourself, that you too may be pure, so as to benefit from the Priest's Mass.

The Priest then petitions the saints to advance his cause. He unites his insufficiency and weakness to their merits. He asks their intercession with God that he may be cleansed of all defilement from past sins. While saying this last prayer, the Priest kisses the altar. The altar stone, containing the relics of saints, represents Christ, the total Christ; that is, all the faithful united to Christ--the whole glorified Mystical Body.

Here is the altar of the saints--the Heavenly Altar of the Apocalypse (Apoc 8:12). Here, Christ makes meaningful and eternally worthwhile the *sacrificial oblations* of the Elect. Here the saints are offered to God with Christ, in Christ and through Christ.

Padre Pio kissed this altar with great reverence. Here were the earthly remains of saints who helped Padre Pio to desire and to execute his *total oblation into Christ,* that is, making the Mass so much a part of his life that he became the first stigmatist-Priest.

THE PRIEST ASCENDS TO THE KINGDOM

The Priest ascends unto the altar. What beautiful symbolism! That's why every church elevated the altar. Where is the altar? The altar is far above us--in the eternal Kingdom of God (Apoc 5:4). Here is where Padre Pio lived--in the Kingdom, through a body in mystical union with, (as well as) in mystical conformity to, the Victim through Whom Salvation comes.

God has chosen him and other men from among us to be *in persona Christi:* in order *to be Christ offering*; in order *to have Christ offered again;* and in order *to give to the Elect Christ, the Holy Eucharist,* as Viaticum--*Food* for their earthly sojourn, an arduous task of living Christ, Christ Crucified. *"Unless you eat the Flesh of the Son of Man, you will not have life in you* (Jo 6:53)." You will be able to live Christ in you--Christ Crucified--only through receiving Christ, the Holy Eucharist. Padre Pio is forever this Priest according to the Order of Melchisedech.

The Priest ascends. He leaves our dimension. He leaves the profane--that which stands before and outside of God's Temple. In the words of the Eastern Rite, the Priest enters into the Kingdom of the Father and of the Son and of the Holy Ghost--

that Kingdom which exists now and forever.

The Priest, a mere mortal, enters into the Kingdom or the Life of God, *through, with and in* the Blood of the Lamb, *which he, (this priest),* is empowered by Christ to offer unto God. He enters the Kingdom because he was validly ordained to celebrate the Holy Sacrifice. As validly ordained, he was singled out to be an alter Christus. With such credentials in hand, he and he alone, ascends unto the Altar of God.

This Priest and only he enters the Kingdom to bring this Kingdom into our space-time for the good of God's Elect; and as St. Paul assures us, for the further condemnation of unredeemed sinners and especially of those who dare to receive Christ, Holy Eucharist, unworthily (1Co 11:29). It is only through the Priest, that the Elect (in spirit and in anticipation) enter into the Kingdom. For all eternity, they will be infinitely grateful for the validly ordained and validly functioning priests, through whom Christ came to them during their earthly lives.

Thank God for priests! Only they can bring the Saving-Action and the Saving-Person into our space-time. Thank God for the Heavenly Gift that priests bring to us. Thank God for Padre Pio--the model for priests who celebrate the Canonized Mass. Thank God, even though any thanksgiving is inadequate. Thank God, for not to thank Him would constitute a gross lack of gratitude and a profanation of the Holy.

YOUR DISPOSITION AT MASS

According to Pope Pius XII, your disposition at Mass should be:

> the disposition of the Divine Redeemer Himself, when He sacrificed Himself--the same humble spirit of submission--that is, of adoration, love, praise and thanksgiving to the great majesty of God...so that you reproduce in yourselves the condition of victimhood, the self-denial that follows the Gospel's teaching, whereby of your own accord you make the willing sacrifice of penance, sorrow and expiation for sins.

True and active participation at Holy Mass is that which makes us into slain victims like Jesus and succeeds in *"reproducing in us the pain-marked features, the suffering likeness of Jesus"* (Pius XII) allowing us *"the fellowship of His sufferings"* as we are *"made conformable to His death"* (Philippians 3:10). As Pope Pius XII uttered these words, there lived in his midst the only stigmatist-priest that has ever lived.

Indeed, He *reproduced Jesus* within himself, Jesus in himself, as "slain victim." St. Gregory the Great taught:

> The Sacrifice of the altar will be on our behalf truly acceptable as our offering to God when we present ourselves as victims. (St. Gregory the Great)

As a reflection of this doctrine, in early Christian communities the faithful used to advance in penitential garb, chanting the litany of the Saints. If we would go to Mass in this spirit, we should want to make our own the sentiment St. Thomas the Apostle expressed when he said, *"Let us also go, that we may die with Him"* (John 11:16). *Dying with Christ* was one of Padre Pio's favorite themes. This theme came from the Canonized Mass.

CHAPTER TEN

GLORIA AND CREDO

"Gloria in excelsis Deo."

GLORY to God in the highest. And on earth, peace to men of good will. We praise Thee. We bless Thee--We speak well of Thee. We adore Thee. We glorify Thee. We give Thee thanks for Thy great glory. O Lord God, heavenly King, God the Father Almighty, O Lord Jesus Christ, the Only-begotten Son, O Lord God, Lamb of God, Son of the Father: Who takest away the sins of the world, have mercy on us. Who sittest at the right hand of the Father, have mercy on us, for Thou alone art holy, Thou alone are the Lord, Thou alone, O Jesus Christ, are most high, together with the Holy Ghost in the glory of God the Father. Amen.

In a positive and active way, glory is the acknowledgement and praise by rational creatures of God's worth. God is to be all in all. God's glory will be shown in all of His creatures.

Authentically, yet negatively, as Padre Pio was well aware, God's glory is shown forth by His justly condemning human souls and fallen angels to an eternal Hell. Either in Heaven or in Hell each will glorify God. Glory to God is inevitable. Glory is now given to God by all. Glory will be forever given to God by all.

God's positive and active glory, as peace, comes only to men of good will. No one is good, but God. Therefore, peace comes only to men of *God-Will*--men who are God oriented, God believing, God graced, God obedient and God chosen.

Men such as these constitute the *we* of the Gloria. The *we* in *we glorify Thee* is clearly that of the Elect. Such a *we* and only such a *we* praise, bless, adore, glorify and give thanks to God in a positive or affirmative manner. The heart of such glorifying of God is the Lamb of God, Son of the Father--*the slain Lamb* of the Apocalypse (Apoc 5:12).

Only He is holy. Only He is Lord. Only He has mercy on repentant sinners. And only He can take away their sins. The Lamb once slain is the essence of Heaven for the Elect. This, the Lamb slain, is Heaven. This, the Lamb slain, is each valid Mass.

How blessed are we who are aware and properly respond to the essence or Heart of Heaven coming into our space and time through God's mysterious divine-transformation. Here at Mass, we confront an open-ended challenge to praise and glorify Christ.

Christ's Sacrifice is the Sacrifice. This is the Source, Sustenance and Summit of the life of God's Elect--both in time, at each valid Mass; and, eternally (cf. Apoc 5:12). We praise, thank and adore Thee, Lord Jesus Christ, the Saviour from sin and Hell.

THE NICENE CREED

"The Lord penetrates into my soul...and the truth speaks of its own accord." (Padre Pio, 8-12-1914)

I BELIEVE in one God, the Father Almighty...And in one Lord Jesus Christ, the Only-begotten Son of God...Who for us men, and for our salvation, came down from heaven (genuflect) and was made Flesh by the Holy Ghost of the Virgin Mary: And was made man. (rise) He was also crucified for us, suffered under Pontius Pilate and was buried. And on the third day He rose again according to the Scriptures. And ascended into heaven, He sits at the right hand of the Father. And He shall come again in glory to judge the living and the dead; and of His kingdom there shall be no end...And I believe in the Holy Ghost...in One, Holy, Catholic and Apostolic Church. I confess one Baptism for the remission of sins. And I look for the resurrection of the dead. And the life of the world to come. Amen.

Here in the creed is contained a summation of some of the God-given Realities or basic tenets in which *each one* is called to believe. *We believe* implies an unreal abstraction. Each believes or doesn't believe. Salutary truth is self-evident or should I say *Faith-evident*? This is so because *"the Lord penetrates my soul"* in such a way that *"the truth speaks of its own accord."*

GOD THE FATHER

Do you believe in the Father? He mirrors Himself among us in all properly functioning fathers--from priests to domestic fathers. If you don't honor fathers you can see, don't claim to honor and respect *the Father*.

God the Father created all. He made you. He made you to know and obey Him and thus to go to Heaven; *or*, you are free to refuse to know Him and/or to disobey Him and thus to go to Hell forever. Out of love, He willed or desired your salvation from eternal Hell. These desires are His Salutary Will toward us or for us. These desires led Him to send us *His Son made Flesh*.

GOD, THE SON AND MARY

The Second Person of the triune, yet one God, was made flesh of (or by) the Holy Ghost *ex Maria Virgine*. Mary is the Mother of Jesus. Jesus is God. Mary is the Mother of God.

Mary is *the perfect human person*. Jesus is *a Divine Person, not a human person*. He assumed a perfect and adorable human nature. Thereby, we can and should adore the Sacred Heart of Jesus. Thereby, we reverence the Immaculate Heart of Mary with like, but not equal sentiments. Padre Pio reverenced Mary. He also became like unto the Mother he loved.

From all eternity, as mirrored in the epistles for *the Immaculata* (celebrated on December 8--one of Padre Pio's favorite Masses), God loved Mary fully. She and she alone, was and is perfectly transparent to Divinity. She and she alone, among human people was boundlessly lovable. She is unique. She is the key participant in the drama of salvation. As it were, the infinite love or God-force met this one and only perfectly cooperative finite person. What resulted is the Elect of Heaven. *"Woman, behold your son!" "Son, behold your mother."* Here on the cross, Jesus disclosed Mary's place in our redemption.

Our joy is Mary being one of us humans. Any of the Elect goes to Heaven because of Jesus' love of the one and only perfect human person. Thus, one goes to Jesus through the Blessed Virgin Mother. She is *full of grace*--the channel of all salutary graces, as the Greek original implies.

God can't directly love sin or sinners within whom sin resides. God loved Mary and through His love of her, He brought into being and loved the rest of the Elect. God loves Mary fully and without reserve. God the Saviour comes to the Elect *because of and from* His love of Mary. Now, as always, Christ's Salutary Deed and Salutary Presence comes to us through Mary.

St. Maximilian Kolbe, a saint of the twentieth century, informs us that as Christ's human nature is to the Second Person, so is Mary to the Holy Ghost. What depths of devotion open to us from such a revelation. Indeed, *de Maria numquam satis--we can never praise and thank Our Lady enough.*

THE JUDGE COMETH

The Judge is coming. Jesus will return to judge you and me according to His standards. In most cases, because of men's sins, His standards won't be the average person's standards. Guess who will win for all eternity?

Agonize to know God's Revelations--to know the dogmas and morals which come to us from Christ. Reject any and all edicts or even suggestions which are alien to Apostolic Tradition. Cling to your common-sense understanding of binding *semper ubique idem* (always and everywhere the same) Catholic Dogma or morals (rules for men relating to God in liturgy and for man rightly relating to himself or others in personal or social life).

The test for contemporary Catholics is to discover

and expose ecclesial deception and to reject it or to go along with popular deceptions and thus be damned to eternal Hell along with the many deceivers and the many, many deceived. Work out your salvation from Hell most carefully. Remember that the odds are against you. Our Lady tells us that *many go to Hell.*

Narrow is the path to Heaven. Few find this path and even fewer travel the path to its completion. So states Jesus in His Bible (Mt 7:14). Therefore, *agonize* to enter Heaven (Lu 13:24 as the original Greek states). *Agonize,* as did Padre Pio. Let him inspire and help you to get to Heaven by living, *not you but Christ-Crucified.*

PRESUMPTION ISN'T HOPE

Et expecto resurrectionem mortuorum. Et vitam venturi saeculi. Amen. By God's grace, attain and retain the virtue of Hope. Refuse to pleasantly presume.

Convinced they are hope-filled, yet rejecting the

true virtue of Hope, many of the deceived embrace the demonic delusion of presumption. Presumption is the assured pleasant delusion that one will not go to Hell. *God's too good to send anyone to Hell...God loves unconditionally.*

Hope is the God-given conviction that if one lives as God revealed through His Church, in the manner prescribed to attain Heaven, one will be judged by Christ to go to Heaven--by God's graces, of course. Note well the difference between popular presumption and the scarcely held virtue of Hope. Then, abandon or carefully avoid the popular delusion--presumption--which leaves out the *big if* in the definition of Hope.

Do you believe? Do you believe the popularly rejected essentials such as, for example: outside the Church, there is no salvation; the dedicated celibate state is superior to the married state; the Mass is the Holy Sacrifice; the tenets of the Natural Law--which decree that abortion, divorce, pre-marital sex and contracepting are Mortal Sins?

What are your Catholic devotions? Are you devoted to the Holy Sacrifice of the Mass, to Mary, to Roman Catholicism and to the *semper ubique idem* Catholic Church?

If you resolve to imitate Padre Pio, live so that the Lord may penetrate into your soul. Then, the truth will speak to you of its own accord. Consequently, you will believe unto your salvation from Hell into Heaven.

CHAPTER ELEVEN

LEX ORANDI LEX CREDENDI

Before entering the *substance of the Mass,* become more convinced that you need this prayer--the Mass prayer. To pray is to lift, and have lifted (by God) one's mind and heart to God, but *not* as understood by average man-centered individuals in contemporary society.

Such an understanding presumes that each human can decide to pray and consequently, that he will pray. However, man can't pray on his own. His attempt to meritoriously lift his mind to God is futile. Man, on his own, simply cannot do so.

You may think: I often lift up my mind and heart to a concept which I label as being *God.* However, are you praying? Are you lifting up your mind and heart to *the God* or to a false god?

You and I naturally are inclined to pray as *we decide.* For example, this attitude is expressed in the currently popular adage *one religion is as good as any other* or *do what you think is right and you'll go to Heaven.* More importantly, this attitude is expressed in the rejection of the Holy Sacrifice of the Mass itself!

As we have seen, the first salutary intervention of God towards Adam and his helpmate (whose sinful conniving soured her into Adam's sin-mate) was to clothe them with animal skins. These animal skins came *from the death or sacrifice of an animal.* They pointed to (as do a millenium of God-appointed Judaic animal sacrifices) *the One Holy Sacrifice of Christ: realized in the First Mass and actualized on Calvary; realized in every valid Mass; and in eternal Heaven.*

The Holy Sacrifice is the Heart or essence of Heaven--*the Lamb slain* (Apoc 5:11-14). The Holy Sacrifice makes prayer possible. The Holy Sacrifice is prayer's needed element coming to us in our present time--*from the future*--as an anticipation for the Elect and from the past by totally (as totally as God can bring about by His Divine Transformation) *re-present-ing* the Calvary-Sacrifice of Good Friday.

*His Broken Body, our only Food. His
Shed Blood, our only Drink. Because of
which we call this Friday Good.*

The Holy Sacrifice is Heaven's Prayer--the Heart of Heaven. As it were, this is the needed and sufficient element to make our naturally God-less eternity into a personal Heaven of boundless and endless unspeakable joy. Likewise, this is the element needed to make any life positive to God.

In the endless now of eternity, prayer is fully realized in each of the Elect. It is realized by the Holy Sacrifice--*the Lamb slain* (Apoc 5:4). Since this is true, how can anyone escape Hell if he neglects or distorts *so great Salvation?* (Hb 2:3).

The great sign of one's election is that one knows, appreciates and loves the Holy Sacrifice, the Mass. The great sign of election is to strive to pray and live the Mass in the piety of Padre Pio.

Lex orandi, lex credendi--the way one prays determines his beliefs. What one believes or fails to believe determines the modality of his eternal existence--in Heaven or in Hell.

This law is illustrated in the words and thoughts of Padre Pio. He acquired his mindset from the prayers of the Holy Sacrifice of the Mass--the Mass instituted by Christ for priests to celebrate and for laymen to attend *unto salvation from Hell.* This Mass produces a salutary mindset. Such a mindset formed in Padre Pio and was reflected by him.

PADRE PIO'S MINDSET

Padre Pio's mindset was and remains the *semper ubique idem* mindset of the Catholic Church--the mindset of Christ's Holy Sacrifice (Php 2:5). Padre Pio was close to the suffering Saviour. Padre Pio *suffered through, in and into the suffering Saviour.*

> We must keep the *eye of faith* fixed on Jesus Christ Who climbs the hill of Calvary loaded with His Cross, and as he treads painfully up the steep slope of Golgotha, we should see Him followed by an immense throng of souls carrying their own crosses and treading the same

path. Oh, what a beautiful sight is this! Let us fix our mental gaze firmly on it. We see close behind Jesus our most holy Mother, who follows Him perfectly, loaded with her own cross. Then come the Apostles, Martyrs, Doctors, Virgins and Confessors. (From the Letters)

CHAPTER TWELVE

PADRE PIO'S OFFERTORY

"The Holocaust, the Prayer...." (Padre Pio)

To what purpose do you offer Me the multitude of your victims? saith the Lord. I desire not holocausts of rams, and fat of fatlings and blood of calves and lambs and buck goats (Isa 1:11).

As every other priest does and will do until the end of time, Padre Pio, *in persona Christi,* offered Christ, not bread or wine. **HANC IMMACULATAM HOSTIAM**--this Spotless Victim Christ is offered to God, present in the Tabernacle. *Nothing else is acceptable to God unto our salvation from Hell into Heaven.*

Lifting the host on the paten, the Priest says: *SUSCIPE sancte Pater, omnipotens aeterne Deus, hanc immaculatam Hostiam, quam ego indignus famulus tuus offero tibi, Deo meo vivo et vero, pro innumerabilibus peccatis, et offensionibus, et negligentiis meis, et pro omnibus circumstantibus, sed et pro omnibus fidelibus Christianis vivis atque defunctis: ut mihi et illis proficiat ad salutem in vitam aeternam.*

*ACCEPT, O Holy Father, Almighty and Eternal God, the **Immaculate Victim** Whom I, Thy unworthy servant, offer unto Thee, to atone for my numberless sins, offenses, and negligences; on behalf of all here present and likewise for all faithful Catholics, living and dead, that it may profit me and them unto birth into eternal life.*

Christ became man, suffered the Holy Sacrifice of Calvary, and is present to us now in each valid Holy Sacrifice of the Mass in order to bring each properly disposed person *ad salutem in vitam aeternam*--to salvation into eternity. *Accept, O Holy Father, Almighty and Eternal God, this Immaculate Victim, Jesus Christ.* Not bread, nor wine, neither worthless gold nor worthless unredeemed sinful humanity, is offered to God the Father.

CHRIST--the Second Person Who assumed human nature--offers HIMSELF to God the Father. *He Who is God* and *God-man* offers and is offered at every valid Mass. HE and HE alone is HANC IMMACULATAM HOSTIAM. Yet, another Immaculate Victim was also at Calvary. The Blessed Virgin Mary was at Calvary.

In the closest union possible for any creature, Mary somehow offered herself along with Christ to the Heavenly Father. Somehow, at each Mass, as it were, Our Lady, along with; totally dependent upon; and, subservient to Christ, is also offered to God the Father.

"The Lord Jesus is with thee"--the Annunciation. Mary is the blessed woman, the immaculate human person, the Immaculata, the God-chosen replacement for Eve. Mary was to Jesus as Eve should have been to Adam.

According to the Colossians' Mystery, even the ordinary Elect person is able to participate in saving souls. If this is true for ordinary humans, how much more is this true for Our Lady, our tainted nature's solitary boast--the *only sinless human person?*

When the Immaculate Victim is offered, primarily, Jesus the Immaculate Victim and, secondarily, Mary the Immaculata, are both offered in sacrifice. With what unspeakable agony and great love did Mary birth her children!

When the Immaculate Victim (Immaculata Hostiam) is offered to God the Father, *Mary* (the principal beneficiary and dependent co-Victim) *is offered with Jesus, the Immaculate Victim,* by the Priest. Both the IMMACULATE VICTIM as *Source of all graces* and the Immaculata as the *fountain of all graces* are offered in different ways *to birth the Elect into being.*

No wonder the Stigmatist-Priest, Padre Pio, was so devoted to Mary. He was so devoted that he became like unto her. Padre Pio lived the Colossians' Mystery (Col 1:25). He brought about the salvation from Hell of many souls. He increased the number of the Elect.

ONLY THE PRIEST

Only the validly ordained Priest, *in persona Christi,* offers Christ. *Ego indignus famulus tuus offero tibi Deo meo vivo et vero.* The Priest and the Priest alone says or celebrates Mass. He does not need *the community* to say his Mass.

The Priest, as Christ, offers the Holy Sacrifice *pro innumerabilibus peccatis, et offensionibus, et negligentiis meis...*for the forgiveness of his own sins. Each Priest, as *father*, represents me to God. Therefore, the holier he is, the better it is for me.

The Priest, as Christ, offers the Immaculate Victim: *pro omnibus circumstantibus* (for those here present) *sed et pro omnibus fidelibus christianis* (for all faith-filled Catholics). The Priest needs no congregation. He acts *in persona Christi* for all faithful Catholics.

The Holy Sacrifice saves the Elect. Here, each prays that he is or will be one of the Elect. Each Mass is offered to obtain *salus in vitam aeternam*--salvation for all eternity. Each Mass is the Holy

Sacrifice *re-presented*. The Holy Sacrifice made present again is the Source of Salutary graces or the means to be saved. By divine transformation, Good Friday comes into our midst to bring into existence God's holy people--just as the Holy Sacrifice brings about the Sacrament Most Holy.

WATER AND WINE

> Don't pray at Holy Mass, but pray *the* Holy Mass...the highest prayer that exists...You have to associate your heart with the holy feelings which are contained in the Priest's words, and in this manner, you ought to follow all that happens on the Altar. When acting in this way, you have prayed the Holy Mass. (His Holiness Pope St. Pius X)

The Priest...pours wine and after blessing the water, pours water also into the chalice. The significance of mingling water with wine and *not blessing the wine, whereas he blesses the water*, is explained by St. Thomas.

Water ought to be mingled with the wine which is offered in this sacrament. First of all, on account of its institution, for it is believed that our Lord instituted this sacrament in wine tempered with water according to the custom of that country (Prov 1:5). Secondly, because it harmonizes with the representation of our Lord's Passion. Hence Pope Alexander I says: 'In the Lord's chalice neither wine only, nor water only ought to be offered, but both mixed because we read that both flowed from His side in the Passion.

The shedding of the blood belonged directly to Christ's Passion; for it is natural for blood to flow from a wounded human body. But the flowing of the water was not necessary for the Passion; but merely to show its effect, which is to wash away sins and to refresh us from the heat of concupiscence. (Summa theol., q.74. A.6)

This is adapted for signifying the effect of this sacrament, since as Pope Julius says:

> We see that the faithful are signified by the water, but Christ's blood by the wine. Therefore, when water is mixed with the wine in the chalice, the faithful 'being blessed' are signified as being one with Christ. (Council. Bracarens, III, canon 1.) (Summa theol., IIIa, q.74. a.6)

We have the symbolism of *our* water being mixed with Christ's wine. We bring a drop of water. It must be BLESSED into becoming worthy to partake of and unite with the wine, Christ.

That's all we are. That's all we bring--a drop of water transformed in order to become one with the wine, Christ. Only then does this drop become symbolic of the Elect's part in Christ's Sacrifice and of the Elect's participation in Christ's *Blood-won* Life--both now and especially, in Heaven. This drop is mixed with the wine. It is no more. Yet, it still exists. Only wine remains. As seldom before, this sign or symbolism was realized in one person--Padre Pio.

Convinced of this symbolism and believing wholeheartedly in the truth behind it, Padre Pio once chastised an overzealous layman. This layman had complimented him on his sufferings for us. Padre Pio was disturbed. He corrected this compliment by pointing out that his sufferings [in themselves] were of absolutely no value. As it were, the drop of water must be *annihilated into wine* in order to be worthwhile. Alluding to this symbolism, the holy Cardinal Mercier once wrote as follows:

> I am the tiny drop of water absorbed by the wine of the Mass, and the wine of the Mass becomes the Blood of the God-Man. And the God-Man is substantially united to the Most Holy Trinity. The tiny drop of water is carried away into the river of life of the Holy Trinity...Will it ever be pure enough, limpid enough, this tiny drop of water destined to participate in the Holy Sacrifice of the Mass? (Cardinal Mercier)

The Priest, *in persona Christi,* and in Christ's name with His power, blesses this little drop, thus symbolizing that Christ has chosen the Elect on earth to be blessed--to be totally metamorphasized or transformed and purified so as *to be part of* or *participate in Christ's sacrifice.*

> The heart of Jesus and my own--allow me to use the expression--were fused... My own heart had disappeared, as a drop of water is lost in the ocean. (Letters, 18-4-1912)

While he mixes the drop of water with the wine, the Priest fittingly prays as follows:

> *O God, Who established the nature of man in wondrous dignity, and still more admirably restored it, grant that through the mystery of this water and wine, we may be made partakers of His Divinity.*

Recall that the grapes had to be crushed in a winepress. Christ has trodden the winepress alone (Isa 63:3). He alone is both the Offerer and the Offered. The best any of us can be is to become blessed so as to offer and to be offered through, with and in Christ.

As it were, by Christ's grace and mercy, we

merely join Christ in His accomplished work. All of man's natural or solitary deeds are *per se* filthy trash (Isa 64:6). With this in mind, in a contrite and humble spirit, let us always marvel that the wine, Christ, doesn't reject us, the water.

However, THE MYSTERY OF FAITH isn't that simple. Only the chosen few are BLESSED to join Christ-Crucified and to be like unto Him. These *make up in their bodies what is lacking of the sufferings of Christ in their bodies for the sake of His body, the Church.* This is the correct translation of Colossians' 1:24, from the Greek. Padre Pio lived this mystery as very few others ever did.

UNLEAVENED BREAD

The Colossians' Mystery is also symbolized by the unleavened bread. Each of the Elect who lives for any length of time as an adult must become crucified through, in and into Christ. Before becoming bread, individual grains of wheat must be milled, crushed and passed through

119

the fire. Each must be crushed, fired and baked in the fires of tribulation and suffering.

Christ has chosen each of His Elect. Together, they form His One Mystical Body just as together the grains form one circular piece of bread.

This wheat is unleavened--not mixed with the yeast of decay, which emanates from the flesh (living for one's natural self) and from the world (living for or from another or a community of men). Only pure or unleavened grains can be metamorphasized or *transformed from within* into *that* which to all appearances is still bread but which is the Body of Christ.

The Elect look like others, just as *consecrated bread* looks like *un*consecrated bread. However, the Elect are totally different. They live, not them, but Christ in them, just as after the consecration, the bread is destroyed and HOC is brought into being: *HOC is My Body.*

Offero...Hanc Immaculatam Hostiam--the Priest and he alone offers in sacrifice the Immaculate

Victim--*not bread and wine.* He does so before the words of Consecration because the Mass is the ongoing Saving-Will of Christ--to offer and to be offered for sinners.

The Mass--all of the Priest's words, deeds and intentions, form a single unit. St. Thomas reflects this Catholic truth as he points out that *all of the words of the Canon determine the FORM.*

The Leonine principle--through the application of which Anglican Orders and services were declared *invalid*--extended this Thomistic Law. Not only did *all of these words determine the form,* they also, as interpreted by common sense-- *determined the intention.* This intention was judged to *invalidate Anglican orders* (and thus, services) by Pope Leo XIII in 1896.

Christ's Saving-Will, by the words, deeds and intentions of validly ordained and validly functioning priests, is realized in our midst at the Holy Sacrifice. This Sacrifice is so God-powerful that the fullness of Christ's Saving-Presence among us--the Sacrament Most Holy--is brought about. *Here* is the Mystery of Faith, which is believed by those who have salutary faith.

Indeed, the Canonized Mass constitutes a flawless diamond. To significantly alter it is to destroy it. The theology of the Mass and its character as Holy Sacrifice is far deeper than you or I perceive. We have merely scratched the surface, yet the little we perceive testifies to the folly and sacrilege of changing the Canonized Latin Mass in any way. Remember that Padre Pio's perception of the Mass was so far superior that, he suffered the Holy Sacrifice of Mass in the wounds of his body.

THE OFFERING

OFFERIMUS tibi, Domine, calicem salutaris tuam deprecantes clementiam: ut in conspectu divinae majestatis tuae, pro nostra et totius mundi salute cum odore suavitatis ascendat. Amen.

WE OFFER to Thee, O Lord, THE CHALICE OF SALVATION seeking Thy loving mercy that it may benefit us and others unto salvation from Hell. Amen.

The prayers of offering will climax in the *Quam oblationem,* which can be personalized as follows:

O God, make Christ-Oblation through and in me, acceptable to Thee, so that Christ will dwell in me forever.

Christ alone is offered to God the Father. My only hope is to be offered through (or into) and in Christ, and thus, to participate in the Mass. Jesus Christ is offered to God. Through and in Christ, the Elect are offered to God--potentially or actually; now and forever, at each Canonized Mass. I can be offered only in and through the Sacrifice. I, being crucified through and in Christ, will become eternal oblation in the Heavenly Sacrament, Christ glorified.

The Mass is a sacrifice. Offering sacrifice is a priestly act. The laity, then, share in the priesthood of Christ, (called by Pope Pius XII *the priesthood of the laity*) **only if there is a sacrifice**

for them to offer, since they cannot produce a sacrifice. Only an ordained priest can do so this side of death.

Likewise, those laymen attending Mass who are said to share in Christ's priesthood, *can participate in the Holy Sacrifice here and now only through a priest.* Laymen may participate in Mass, but need a validly ordained priest to provide the Mass. It is the Priest's highest function and privilege to offer sacrifice. Only priests have Christ's priestly power. This is why priests exist. This is why Padre Pio existed.

A parallel problem suggests itself. Just as the Cains among us purpose to go to Heaven *as they choose*, so also do these Cains among us presume to change Christ's Sacrifice and Sacrament into *the liturgy as they choose.*

Offerimus tibi calicem. By God's mysterious and infinite love, you too, can offer--through the Priest who acts or offers *in persona Christi*, your *Christ-ed* self to God the Father. You can be part of that *we who offer--the Offerimus.*

By offering the chalice, the chalice of salvation which is the chalice of your *Christ-ed* suffering, you become part of the *Offerimus*. Whenever Christ lives in anyone this side of death, He does so to suffer or to be crucified. He does so to offer Himself *in them.*

How well did Padre Pio know this! How greatly did Padre Pio love this! How very much did Padre Pio desire this as he prayed this very *offerimus* at every one of his Masses! How very much did Padre Pio realize this in his life, a life made by the Holy Sacrifice of the Mass--a life within which Christ lived so as to offer Himself and Padre Pio *in Him* to God the Father.

If you so choose to be part of the Offertory and in as much as you are part of the Offertory, you offer and are offered as, *calicem salutaris,* the chalice of salvation, the chalice of much personal suffering. At the very least, you must die to your flesh (the natural desires of your body and mind) and die to the world (living for another person or other people) and you must live as Christ demands. To do so, you will need the power of grace which comes from the Mass. In doing so, you will somehow and somewhat become part of the Sacrifice, part of the Mass.

Our Lady challenged her very little children at Fatima: *Will you accept out of true love the chalice of much sufferings, which Our Lord will give you in order to save other souls and to console the Sacred Heart and my own Immaculate Heart?*

Here, in sacrifice, is how you participate in Mass. Here is how you pray *offerimus*. As Pope St. Pius X and other saints, as well as the official and binding *semper et ubique idem* (always and everywhere the same) Church defines *participation--to die to your flesh and the world; and to live as Christ demands.*

THE EFFECTS OF OFFERIMUS

Tuam deprecantes clementiam--we pray to obtain your great mercy or clemency; *ut in conspectu divinae majestatis tuae*--that in your Divine

Presence (in Heaven); *cum odore suavitatis*--there may arise a pleasing fragrance; *pro nostra, et totius mundi salute*--which may avail unto our salvation and as much as can be made possible by our *offerimus* realized, the salvation even of the whole world.

We pray *pro totius mundi*--for the whole world, although the whole world is not saved. All men are not part of the Holy Sacrifice. We are reminded of every man's opportunity to be saved and to remind ourselves of our opportunity to partake in the sufferings of Christ. If each Catholic suffered as God desires, (I'm convinced) the whole world would be saved. We know that the Holy Sacrifice is the Effective Sacrifice (according to the binding dogmatic teachings of Florence, Trent and other Catholic decrees) only for a multitude (multis) which is very far from being *all*.

If each Catholic attending Mass, had the mind and heart of St. Paul and lived as he lived, perhaps, all would be saved. Remember the Colossians' Mystery: *I strive to fulfill in my body what is lacking of the sufferings of Christ in my body, for the sake of His Body, the Church* (Eph 1:24).

A CLEANSED OFFERING

I will wash my hands among the innocent, and I will encompass Thine Altar, O Lord...I have walked in my innocence; redeem me, and have mercy on me.

Symbolically, the Priest washes his hands to indicate that he wishes to perform this sacrifice more fruitfully, and therefore, should be free from sins as best he can be. His prayers show him and us that nothing less than total purity of soul should be his and ours.God's Sacrifice demands our sacrificial cooperation. Regarding the spiritual meaning of the washing of the fingers, St. Cyril of Jerusalem wrote:

> This action shows that the priest must be free from all sin. It is his hands which have done these things; to wash his hands is the nearest thing to purifying his deeds. (St. Cyril of Jerusalem)

Referring to Pontius Pilate's action before condemning Jesus to crucifixion, a religious author wrote:

> Let us take good care that each one of us can say in all truth 'I am innocent of the Blood of Jesus Christ.'

LAVABO INTER INNOCENTES

This *Lavabo* recalls to mind the priests of the millenium of preparation--the priests of God's Old Dispensation. They washed at the *laver* which was in the major courtyard of the Temple--the only place of God's special presence on earth. The Temple was on Mt. Calvary. The priests of the Old Testament washed at Calvary. Now, O priest, you wash to be as worthy as you can of being Christ at Calvary.

God required *innocence* of His priests who sacrificed in His sight, the blood of animals and the loaves of wheat. What severely ascetical lives they led and for what--mere shadows of (and preparation for) the Prayer, the Holy Sacrifice.

However, it was indeed right and totally just that God demanded purity of His priests of a thousand years. How much more does He demand of His priests who offer The Holy Sacrifice?

How blessed are you--validly ordained priest. You act or do *in persona Christi.* You and you alone celebrate Mass. No one else does. You walk around God's altar, before that which infinitely surpasses the Holy of Holies--into which Old Testament priests would venture only with utmost caution, reverence and holy fear. Each Priest prays as Padre Pio prayed:

> I am in Thy Sanctuary, O God. I am here to be as Christ: offering Christ; sacrificing Christ; receiving Christ; and giving Christ to my flock. Here I am, Lord, so close to Calvary--Calvary made present as I say a valid Mass. Glory to Thee, O Lord. Glory to Thee, now and always.

OBLATION

"What distresses me the most is that I repay Jesus' love with so much ingratitude." (Padre Pio)

SUSCIPE, sancta Trinitas, hanc oblationem quam tibi offerimus ob memoriam passionis, resurrectionis et ascensionis Jesu Christi Domini nostri: et in honorem beatae Mariae semper Virginis, et beati Joannis Baptistae, et sanctorum Apostolorum Petri et Pauli, et istorum, et omnium Sanctorum: ut illis proficiat ad honorem nobis autem ad salutem: et illi pro nobis intercedere dignentur in coelis, quorum memoriam agimus in terris. Per eumdem Christum Dominum nostrum. Amen.

Returning to the middle of the Altar, the celebrant raises his eyes to Heaven toward the Crucifix. With a humble and recollected attitude, he lowers them toward the Altar. With his hands joined on the edge of the Altar, he renews the act of offering in these translated words:

Receive, most Holy Trinity, the Oblation offered up to Thee in memory of the Passion, Resurrection, and Ascension of our Lord Jesus Christ...and in honor of Blessed Mary, ever Virgin, Blessed John the Baptist, the Holy Apostles Peter and Paul, and of these and all the saints that it may avail to their honor and aid our salvation; and may they, who are now part of The Memory which is re-done on earth (at valid Masses) deign to intercede for us.

This prayer should elicit a yearning from you to be oblated into The Memory--the sufferings of Christ or Christ suffering in you. Such an oblation will save souls--yours and others. Such oblation will honor the saints who are even now partakers of The Memory or the Mystery of Faith. The Mystery of Faith is coming to your here and now. The Memory will be re-done at this valid Mass.

Pray, sinner. Pray to be part of the Oblation. Pray to Mary that she may pray for you, now and at the hour of your death. Pray to all saints who are part of the Oblation. May those in whose honor the Christ-Oblation is offered, remember you in a special way. Petition Jesus that you may be part of The Oblation. It is only through being part of The Oblation that you will be effected into the Memoria of Christ for all eternity in Heaven.

OB MEMORIAM

The Oblation is effected or brought into being and sustained only through Jesus Christ. *Ob memoriam passionis, resurrectionis et ascensionis Jesus Christi, Domini nostri*--from being brought into the Memory of the passion, resurrection and ascension of Our Lord, Jesus Christ is this accomplished. *Memory* is one's life, now and consequently, forever.

All that you are, or I am, for all eternity, is our memory--the summation of our moral decisions. That's you. That's me. That's each of us, as it were, *raised to the infinite power.*

However, since we are sinners naturally damned

to Hell (as the absence of the Beatific Vision, with or without pain), our memories, naturally speaking, are trash. The only way *trash* can be made eternally valuable is by being blessed or totally metamorphasized. Trash must be destroyed. Trash must die. Only then can trash be worthwhile. Likewise, only by dying through, in and into Christ Crucified can you or I be incorporated from and into *the Memory--the life, death and resurrection of Our Lord and Saviour, Jesus Christ.*

OB MEMORIAM PASSIONIS RESURRECTIONIS ET ASCENSIONIS

If you are one of the Elect, then in as much as you now partake of the sufferings of Christ, so much will you be part of Christ's eternal glorification (1 Pet 4:13). Christ's life, sufferings and eternal glorification constitute the entirety or fullness of The Memory--the Memory into which each of the Elect now thankfully partakes; or The Memory into which each of us prays to be made partaker now and forever.

This is your open-ended challenge and the only worthwhile opportunity you have. Agonize to find and to enter the narrow door--the Mystery of Faith. Agonize to walk the arduous narrow path to your final Calvary-death. Agonize in order to *partake of the Memory*--as Christ living in you unto your death to your flesh and to this world; and in obedience to God's will. Agonize now, in order to be an eternal partaker of the eternal glory of The Memory, Jesus Christ.

To pray (and as a priest, to celebrate or say) the Holy Sacrifice is to be assimilated into the Holy Sacrifice. Mt. Tabor can be reached only by properly climbing Mt. Calvary.

> **One day we will know what value and what treasures our earthly sufferings have been that have made us gain our everlasting homeland. From generous souls in love with God, He expects heroic deeds and faithfulness (in order) to arrive at Tabor (only) after the climb to Calvary.** (Padre Pio, Letters)

CHAPTER THIRTEEN

SANCTUS! SANCTUS! SANCTUS!

"During Mass, all of Paradise descends on the altar." (Padre Pio)

Now and forever, the same cry is uttered by Heavenly Powers: *Holy, Holy, Holy is the Lord God of hosts; all the earth is full of His glory* (Is 6:1-3). On earth, His Saving Presence dwells. The Sanctus is called the Seraphic Hymn, because it is sung by the Seraphim. Because he loved Christ and sang His praises ardently like a seraph, St. Francis was also called *seraphic.*

After the celebrant has declared his intention to unite our voices with those of the angels, he inclines moderately and rejoins his hands, which up to now had been extended shoulder level at his sides. Then, as if weighed down by the grandeur of his office, as well as by the sentiment of his unworthiness, he slightly lowers his voice and recites the Sanctus. St. Thomas points out the two-fold aspect of this prayer when he says:

The priest devoutly praises Christ's Godhead, saying with the angels: 'Holy, Holy, Holy; and His humanity, saying with the children: Blessed is He that comes.' (Summa theol., IIIa, q.83, a.4)

This *Sanctus* reminds us that since the Priest's prayer of the Mass is Christ's prayer, it brings us into Heaven even as it brings Heaven to us. *Holy, Holy Holy!* St. Ambrose explains the reason why the word is repeated thrice:

The threefold acclamation expresses God's unity and the Trinity of the Divine Persons. The Seraphim do not sing the word, 'holy' merely once so as not to indicate a solitary Deity. They do not sing it only twice, so as not to exclude the Holy Ghost. They do not sing it in the plural, because there is one God, not several. They repeat it thrice, and this in an identical manner, so that the hymn may help us to understand the distinction and equality of the Divine Persons, as well as their unity of nature. (St. Ambrose)

The apostle St. John, transported in spirit to Heaven, saw and heard, as did Isaias, the angels surrounding God's throne, chanting day and night without ceasing, this same hymn:

> Holy, Holy, Holy, the Lord, God Almighty, Who was, and Who is and Who is coming! (Apoc 4:8)

Deus sabaoth--Lord God of hosts. In acclaiming the Lord here as *Lord God of Hosts,* we refer to the angelic militia mentioned by Daniel the prophet:

> A thousand thousand they were that waited on His bidding, and for every one of these, a thousand others were standing there before Him. (Dan 7:10)

Pleni sunt caeli et terra gloria tua--the heavens and the earth are full of Thy glory. We praise and glorify the Creator, whose attributes shine forth in all that is in the Heavens and on earth: the heavens with their countless suns; the earth, chosen despite its small size, to manifest the marvels of His infinite mercy; to be watered with the Blood of Christ and to become the dwelling-place of the Holy Eucharist--accomplished by the Priest, *in persona Christi,* who recreates Christ's Sacrifice at Holy Mass!

Hosanna in excelsis! Hosanna in the highest! Hosanna is an Hebraic acclamation, borrowed from the 118th Psalm. It means *save us.*

Benedictus qui venit in nomine Domini--Blessed is He Who comes in the name of the Lord. Blessed be Jesus, our Saviour! He is about to descend on the Altar. Let us rejoice and be glad like the Hebrews who went to Jerusalem to see Christ make His triumphal entry. Like them, let us shout *Hosanna! Save me, O Lord. Save me.* Soon, very soon, His Holy Sacrifice and Holy Eucharist will again be made present--will be *re-presented.*

The Eucharistic Sacrifice is the sacrifice of thanksgiving. Be thankful to God for this sign of your election--the free gift of this valid Mass. All we can do and must do is to give and to be Eucharist--thanksgiving.

139

CHAPTER FOURTEEN

TE IGITUR...MEMENTO

"Comprehend the tremendous Mystery: *God, Victim* for our sins." (Padre Pio)

The first prayer of the *Canon:*

> *TE IGITUR, clementissime Pater, per Jesum Christum Filium tuum, dominum nostram, supplices rogamus, ac petimus, (He kisses the Altar) uti accepta habeas, et benedicas haec dona, haec munera, haec sancta sacrificia illibata: in primis, quae tibi offerimus pro Ecclesia tua sancta catholica: quam pacificare, custodire, adunare, et regere digneris toto orbe terrarum: una cum famulo tuo Papa nostro N...et Antistite nostro N...et omnibus orthodoxis, atque catholicae et apostolicae fidei cultoribus.*

> *Therefore, because of He Who comes in Thy name, we whose only need is salvation, ask and beseech Thee, most kind Heavenly Father, through Thy Son*

our Lord, that Thou wilt accept and bless into being this oblation: that which Thou hast given to us (haec dona); that which we have developed (haec munera); these material things bread and wine to be metamorphasized into The Holy Sacrifice (haec sancta sacrificia illibata).

We, supplicants, plead and beg Thee, Most Merciful Father. Notice the stark contrast between this prayer to God the Father (which introduces the solemn Canon of Prayers) and the previous parallel prayer to God the Father (which prayer introduced the Offertory Prayers)--the *Suscipe Sancte Pater.*

In the Offertory Prayer, *haec Immaculata Hostia* is offered to God the Father, in anticipation, but yet actually. Such an offering,--Christ's Offering--is automatically acceptable to, and accepted by, God the Father when offered by a valid priest who acts *in persona Christi* at his validly celebrated Mass.

Here, however, we are not dealing with *The*

Immaculate Victim, Christ. Therefore, we must be *supplices*--supplicators, as the Priest representing us says: *rogamus ac petimus*--we plead and we beg. For what do we now plead and beg? Again, I repeat. *We do not plead and beg that Christ, the Immaculate Victim*, be acceptable to God the Father. God forbid such blasphemy on our part. In fact, we plead and beg that *"what"* we desire God the Father to accept and bless *uti accepta habeas et benedicas* be worthy of such-- *through* Christ or because of Christ--*per Dominum nostrum, Jesus Christum.*

MY PRAYER

Through the Priest, *what then* do I beg to be made acceptable to the Most Merciful and Loving Father? *Haec dona, haec munera, haec sancta sacrificia illibata.* What could these words mean?

All that God gave me, all that I have accomplished by His graces--may these be given to God and received by God as holy and acceptable sacrifice. *All that I now am, I offer through, with and in Christ*--to become a holy sacrifice to God the Father. May these *dona et munera--my givens and my accomplishments,* I plead and beg, be acceptable to God *(accepta habeas)*and blessed, re-created or transformed by God *(benedicas)*.

I pray that my *memory* may be transformed by the Blood of Christ, incorporated into Christ's, and thus be made acceptable to God for all eternity. Such was Padre Pio's prayer. May this be your prayer.

May you be made holy so as to be part of *The Holy. Holy to the Holy. One alone is Holy, to the glory of God the Father.* So prays the Eastern Liturgy at Mass.

We are brought back to Genesis and to Pauline theology. Somehow, pray that all of your life may be made holy by God or be re-created by God. God said, *"Light be. Light was. God separated the light from the darkness (Ga 1:1-3)."* Agonize to be part of the Light. Strive to bring others to the Light.

ECUMENICAL ECCLESIA SANCTA

Prior to Vatican II, *ecumenism* referred to *the apostolic endeavor to make the whole world Catholic.* The Mass was Christ's Mass. Where the Mass was, there was Christ. Where the Mass was, there was His Church. Outside of this Church was damnation and darkness. Therefore, zealous Catholics heroically strove to bring the Mass to the whole world. Such zealous Catholics were *ecumenical.*

The Mass by Christ's Will, is the *effective* Salutary Action and the Mass, like the Sacraments, was instituted *by Christ* to give His graces unto eternal salvation only to His Elect. Therefore, in the fifth century, Gelasius (as noted by Jungmann in <u>The Mass of the Roman Rite</u>) observed the established fact that at Mass, *only faithful Catholics were prayed for* and that *the pope claimed the job of being merely the custodian and dispenser of Catholicism and of the Apostolic Faith* (Christ's expressed Will).

Popes claimed Apostolic succession from Peter,

and as temporary and faithful occupants of the Chair of Peter or what is called the Holy See (or the Apostolic See), governed so as to uphold the Faith, which came to each pope from each previous pope all the way back to Peter, and therefore, Christ. The Holy See always recognized the inability of any pope to change what is written in Scripture or what was handed down from Tradition.

Consequently, popes recognized the grave responsibility to uphold the Faith, as the prime duty of the papacy. **Not even the holy popes of those times claimed to be what is today called *living magisterium.***

The Magisterium is defined as *the teaching authority of bishops under the Roman Pontiff, as successor of St. Peter.* (Catholic Dictionary, Fr. John A. Hardon, S.J., Image Books, October, 1985) This teaching authority exists in the present as it did in the past- -in those persons who faithfully execute this function. While the Magisterium is referred to as *ordinary* or *extraordinary*, magisterium is not referred to as *living.*

Adherents of *living magisterium* often submit Apostolic Tradition to re-appraisal and change. The Church teaches that Apostolic Tradition was closed at the death of the last Apostle. The Canonized Mass is the God-related (or liturgical) part of the *morals*, which was once and forever defined by Apostolic Tradition. *All of this and far more* constituted the *stable defined world* within which Padre Pio and all other priests lived--until the revolting sixties.

MEMENTO

MEMENTO, Domine...make us and those for whom we pray, we beseech Thee, O Lord, partakers of The Memory. Memento, Domine...that's all we pray for. Make me now a partaker of Thy Memory. Make me part of Christ-suffering and Christ-dying. Only thus will I be part of The Eternal Memory, the glorified Christ.

Only those with faith and devotion *offer, and are offered in Christ, the Sacrifice.*

*Quorum tibi fides cognita est, et nota devotio pro quibus Tibi offerimus; vel qui Tibi offerunt...*those whose faith and devotion are known to Thee, O God.

THE MYSTERY OF SALVATION

The Offering isn't magic. Each is saved only by faith and devotion--devotion as a life lived united to Christ and in a way acceptable to God. Devotion is faith unto salvation--salutary faith prayed and lived. Faith and devotion are necessary for salvation. However, their existence and effectiveness are known to God alone. All that we do is to pray and *live* the Holy Mass for our own salvation and the salvation of others.

We strive to imitate Padre Pio and other saints who loved the Lord Jesus and emptied themselves by praying and living the Holy Mass unto the salvation of themselves and others. None of us can save himself from eternal Hell. Each needs the Holy Sacrifice, the Mystery of Faith. Here is the only Source of being saved from eternal Hell.

Both we, and those for whom we pray, are salutarily compelled in a certain and real sense to offer *hoc Sacrificium laudis--this Holy Sacrifice* which evokes eternal praise in Heaven (Apoc 5:4) and as such is the eternal Source, Sustenance and Summit of Heaven itself. Even here, *the offering of laymen occurs only through Christ-priest.*

> To participate in the Eucharistic Sacrifice is the chief duty and supreme dignity of the faithful. They should strive to be united as closely as possible with the High Priest...Together with Him and through Him, let them make their oblation, and in union with Him, let them offer up themselves. (Mediator Dei, Pope Pius XII, 1947)

THE PRIORITY OF SALVATION

We don't trivialize God's Gift for any of our present fleshly and worldly needs. The Canonized Liturgy prays *pro redemptione animarum suarum, pro spe salutis.* The Canonized Liturgy prays for salvation from eternal Hell. This is the only real need of each of us. For those on behalf of whom he offered his Masses, this is what Padre Pio prayed (and prays) in all of his children.

Specifically, the Canonized Liturgy prays for the removal of any and all obstacles to eternal salvation--*incolumitatis suae.* The Canonized Liturgy is devoid of banal and trivial offertory petitions.

Are we not now led to join Padre Pio in making heartfelt resolutions to Christ-crucified, to Christ as depicted on the Altar of Sacrifice? *Tibique reddunt vota sua aeterno Deo, vivo et vero*--to Thee, O God, we render vows...to Thee the One and Only Living and True God, the God Who gave us this Holy Sacrifice and Holy Sacrament; as well as, His one and only Church.

God's Greatest Gift--the Canonized Mass--evokes a response. Padre Pio responded in an exemplary way. That's why he is *the Saint of the Canonized Mass.*

CHAPTER FIFTEEN

OBLATION IN THREE PRAYERS

One day when we are able to see the full midday light, we will know what value and what treasures our earthly sufferings have been that have made us gain our everlasting homeland. From generous souls in love with God, He expects heroic deeds and faithfulness (in order) to arrive at Tabor (only) after the climb to Calvary. (Padre Pio, Letters)

COMMUNICANTES, et memoriam venerantes, in primis gloriosae semper Virginis Mariae, Genitricis Dei et Domini nostri Jesu Christi: sed et beatorum Apostolorum ac Martyrum tuorum, Petri et Pauli, Andreae, Jacobi, Joannis, Thomae, Jacobi, Philippi, Bartholomaei, Matthaei, Simonis et Thaddaei: Lini, Cleti, Clementis, Xysti, Cornelii, Cypriani, Laurentii, Chrysogoni, Joannis et Pauli, Cosmae et Damiani: et omnium Sanctorum tuorum;

quorum meritis precibusque condedas, ut in omnibus protectionis tuae muniamur auxilio. Per eumdem Christum Dominum nostrum. Amen.

VENERATING the memories (lives) of the saints and desiring to be united with them--the glorious ever Virgin Mary, Mother of our God and Lord, Jesus Christ; the blessed Apostles and Martyrs, Peter and Paul, Andrew, James, John, Thomas, James, Philip, Bartholomew, Matthew, Simon and Thaddeus, Linus, Cletus, Clement, Sixtus, Cornelius, Cyprian, Lawrence, Chrysogonus, John and Paul, cosmas and Damien, and all Thy saints--grant, O Lord, for the sake of their merits and prayers that in all things we may be guarded and helped by their intercessions on our behalf. Through the same Jesus Christ our Lord. Amen.

This prayer, *Communicantes, et memoriam venerantes...*together with the next two prayers--*Hanc Igitur* and *Quam Oblationem*--concern *your* *oblation.* Somehow, *you are to be oblated through, in and into Christ.* Thus, do you live, not you, but Christ in you. Thus did and does Padre Pio live, not him, but Christ in him.

As the Priest says the *Hanc Igitur,* he places his hands over the offering. Symbolically, he places his hands over bread and wine. Bread and wine are, at best, symbols and holy signs *until a valid Consecration takes place.* As we have seen, the *unconsecrated bread and wine* symbolize the Elect in many ways.

Christ-priest will bless (metamorphasize) the bread and wine. Christ-priest will *destroy* bread and wine and in their place will be Christ, Holy Eucharist. So also will the Elect be blessed, oblated or *destroyed.*

In these oblation prayers, these symbols and holy signs *stand for or represent the oblation of your life--your dying through, in and into Christ or your being crucified in and into Christ,* in obedience to God's Will. As the wine and bread are metamorphasized or transubstantiated, so should you and your proper oblation become, as much as possible, Christ and His Holy Sacrifice. These oblation prayers remind us of Padre Pio. In a most exemplary manner, he expressed and fulfilled these prayers. In fact, one of his favorite words in describing the Mass is *death.* Unless the grain of wheat dies, it remains its natural self. Unless you are crucified with Christ, you remain your natural Hell-bound self.

SAINTS OF GOD: PRAY FOR US; HELP US

*Communicantes...*It would seem that we have a loose gerund on our hands. Where does it belong? Let's find a home for this gerund.

Tibique reddunt vota sua aeterno Deo, vivo et vero, COMMUNICANTES--to Thee, O God, those who live in common unity or in the full realization of community--communicating with God and with each other through Christ in true fellowship--to Thee, O God, these render their (*sua*) eternal allegiance, to Thee, Who art the Living and True God. I think that this is where *communicantes* primarily belongs. It belongs in the previous prayer. However, *communicantes* also finds a home in this prayer. These *communicantes* are *memoriam venerantes*. They are continually adoring the Memory, Christ the Lamb once slain, Who is the Source, Sustenance and Summit of Heaven.

IN PRIMIS, MARIA

In primis, gloriosae semper Virginis Mariae, Genitricis Dei et Domini Nostri Jesu Christi. In the very first and in the *prime* or prototype place is Our Lady, the Virgin, the Mother of God, the Mother of Jesus.

Mary is *the only sinless human person.* God salutarily came to her and through her came to us. She is *in primis.* Without her, there would be no salvation from Hell for any of us sinners. God, we thank Thee for the Blessed Virgin Mary.

Mary attracted God. Primarily, and as *prototype*, she led or attracted God to become man in Jesus of her flesh, in order to open Heaven to her, the only sinless human person. Study the readings that the Church selected to honor her on her major feast days. Then, you will see what the Church thinks of Our Lady.

At the Holy Sacrifice on Calvary, Christ gave us to Mary and gave Mary to us. Here is the link to my salvation from Hell. Here is the link of your salvation from eternal Hell--the *full channel of all of the graces that come to us from Christ.*

How can I attain *so great salvation* if I neglect or disdain Christ's gift of His Mother to me? Let me ratify her as my mother by how I live. *Secondarily,* or through her, I will partake of the Memory now and forever, if, of course, I am one of the Elect.

The only perfectly *divinely feminine* human person met the infinitely loving God. From this union, the salvation of each of the Elect was brought about as she became *the channel of salvation for each of God's Elect in Christ-Jesus. She mothered the Elect.*

As we have considered, according to the thought of St. Maximillian Kolbe, the Holy Ghost operates through the human person, Mary, in a way similar to the way that the Second Person of the Trinity is united to and operates through the human nature of Jesus Christ. Mary is *the human person fully and boundlessly loved by God.*

Hail Mary, the full channel of all of God's graces. So states the original Greek. *Holy Mary, Mother of God, pray for me, a sinner.* Here, in the Hail Mary, once again we discover Padre Pio. He recited hundreds of Hail Marys every day. Through her, *the one and only sinless human person,* comes the Saviour and His Sacrifice. Through Mary, comes the Mass that made Padre Pio. Through Mary, comes the Mass that saves and sanctifies.

Each Holy Sacrifice culminates in Holy Communion. Each Holy Communion brings you and me to Christ and to Mary at Calvary. Remember Padre Pio's view of Holy Communion. For him, Holy Communion called to mind Christ being taken down from the cross and placed in the arms of Mary--the Pieta. *If* Christ is crucified in you, you will finally be placed in the arms of Mary--the Pieta. Let each of your Holy Communions be like unto Padre Pio's. Let your dying *through, in and into Christ* bring you into the arms of Mary--the Pieta.

BE OBLATED

HANC IGITUR oblationem servitutis nostrae, sed et cunctae familiae tuae, quaesumus, Domine, ut placatus accipias: diesque nostros in tua pace disponas, atque ab aeterna damnatione nos eripi, et in electorum tuorum jubeas grege numerari. Per Christum Dominum nostrum. Amen.

Do Thou, O Lord, be pleased to bring about the desired oblation of our lives in and into the Oblation. Grant us Thy divine peace in this life. Grant us salvation from eternal damnation. Number us among the Elect in Heaven eternally. This we ask through Christ our Lord. Amen.

As the Priest, *in persona Christi,* places his hands over the bread and wine which we desire to represent us, he is joining the priests of a thousand years. They, too, placed their hands over millions of animals, thus indicating that each would be sacrificed to God or indicating on Yom Kippur that this one goat would be designated to be the carrier of our sins--the scape-goat--destined to suffer and die.

As the goat was driven out, sins were removed in symbol and in this God-given ritual. Christ fulfills and makes effective that scape-goat. The word *placatus* reminds us of this, not only as regards Christ, but also as regards each adult member of the Elect.

Now, you are under the Priest's hands--under Christ's hands. You are not primarily a scape-goat. You are primarily a designated sacrifice or oblation to God. Through, *in and into* Christ, *the Oblation--the fulfillment and energizer of all that, for which the God-appointed scape-goats once stood.*

You are called to be sacrificed in and into Christ. You are thus given the opportunity in this life to be transformed or metamorphasized into Christ-suffering in you and, as much as possible, for you to live, *not you,* but Christ-suffering in you. Again, we recall our model for this--Padre Pio.

Hanc igitur oblationem servitutis nostrae. Therefore, let this oblation of our lives to Christ... *quaesumus Domine, ut placatus accipias*--we beseech Thee, O Lord, be acceptable to Thee in view of the accomplished pleasing sacrifice of Christ Himself (*placatus*).

WHY BE OBLATED?

Why do you pray that your oblation through, with and in Christ's Holy Sacrifice be accepted by God? *Diesque nostros in tua pace disponas, atque ab aeterna damnatione nos eripi et in electorum tuorum jubeas grege numerari...* so that all of my days, both in time and into eternity, may be lived in Thy peace...so that I may escape eternal Hell and so that I may be numbered among the Elect. Even now, as is exemplified in the life of Padre Pio, peace comes as the assurance that one is fulfilling God's purpose for him: that He is being oblated through and in Christ-suffering.

Again, the Canonized Mass Liturgy addresses the essentials. This liturgy concerns itself with the eternal and not with the temporal or with the world, which at best passes away; and, at worst, is evilmental. This temporal world can be redeemed only by the Mass and then, only by and for those who pray and live the Canonized Mass.

Unless you die with Christ, you can't live with Him. Along with Padre Pio, tell Christ how much you love and wish to love even more His greatest Gift among us, the Canonized Mass.

THE FINAL PRAYER FOR OUR OBLATION

Quam oblationem, tu, Deus, in omnibus quaesumus, benedictam, adscriptam, ratam, rationabilem, acceptabilemque facere digneris: ut nobis Corpus, et

Sanguis fiat dilectissimi Filii tui Domini nostri Jesu Christi.

Humbly, we pray Thee, O God, be pleased to make our Oblation wholly blessed and set apart in order to do Thy will or to be metamorphasized by Thee (*benedictam*). Make our oblation to be proper and acceptable (*rationabilem acceptabilemque*) to Thee in order that (*ut*) the Body and Blood of Thy dearly beloved Son, Our Lord Jesus Christ, may come to be (*fiat*) in us.

We can sense a certain urgency. *Christ is coming.* May we be made proper and acceptable living tabernacles for Jesus in Holy Communion, through our oblation through, *in and into* Christ-crucified. The *Quam Oblationem* is the third part of our oblation prayers. It completes the previous *Hanc Igitur* prayer.

On our behalf, the Priest prays most sincerely that our oblation may be blessed (*benedictam*) or set apart and destroyed in order to be *Christ-ed*: as prescribed by God's Will (*adscriptam*); to be accepted by God (*ratam*); and acceptable (*rationabilem acceptabilemque*) so as to cause the dwelling or tabernacling of Christ, Body and Blood, within us (*ut nobis Corpus et Sanguis fiat dilectissimi Filii tui Domini nostri Jesu Christi*).

This *perfect prayer* reminds us that *the Mass Prayers go back to Apostolic times and were commanded by Christ.* So have our saints and reliable ancient authorities testified; and so has the Church spoken, by its official and binding *canonizing* or making into *the Rule*, these Mass Prayers for its priests, who celebrate Mass in the Latin Rite. These prayers concern *your* oblation in and into Christ. St. Thomas says:

> The priest does not seem to pray here for the Consecration to be fulfilled, but that it may be fruitful in our regard; hence, he says expressively: That it may become 'to us' the body and blood. Again, the words preceding these have that meaning, when he says: Vouchsafe to make this oblation blessed, i.e., according to Augustine 'that we may receive a blessing, namely through

grace;' 'enrolled,' i.e., that we may be incorporated in Christ; 'reasonable' i.e., that we may be stripped of our animal sense; 'acceptable,' i.e., that we who in ourselves are displeasing may, by its means, be made acceptable to His only Son. (St. Thomas Aquinas, Summa Theologica, IIIA, q.83)

CHAPTER SIXTEEN

IN PERSONA CHRISTI

Deign, O Lord, to *consecrate and make holy* these hands by this unction and our *blessing*. Amen. So that what they will *bless* will be *blessed*; what they will *consecrate* will be *consecrated and made holy* in the name of our Lord Jesus Christ. Amen.
(The bishop's prayer, by which Padre Pio was made a priest.)

The Congregation is on its knees. As Padre Pio often did, the Priest bends over the altar to re-enact what belongs to the domain of faith. The great mystery of our holy religion, the Salutary Will of Christ as Eucharistic Sacrifice, is being *re-presented*--made present again. The *Divine Present* comes to us.

Only the ordained Priest celebrates Mass. The Priest's words change bread and wine into Christ's Body and Blood, for *"these words are uttered in the person of Christ"* (Summa theol., IIIa, q. 78, a.4.). St. Thomas speaks: *"Quasi ex persona ipsius Christi loquentis"* (Summa Theo., a.1). As if Christ were speaking in person, the Priest *re-presents in persona Christi,* what took place at Christ's first Mass and that which was consequently *actualized in Blood on Calvary.*

Qui pridie, quam pateretur, accepit panem in sanctas ac venerabiles manus suas, et elevatis oculis in caelum ad te Deum, Patrem suum omnipotentem, tibi gratias agens, benedixit, fregit, deditque discipulis suis, dicens: Accipite, et manducate ex hoc omnes: HOC EST ENIM CORPUS MEUM.

Who, at the beginning of the Day (Good Friday) on which He suffers (into actuality) THE oblation (quam), He took bread into His holy and venerable (adorable) Hands, having lifted up His eyes towards Heaven to Thee, His Almighty Father, GIVING thanks to Thee, BLESSED, broke and gave [HOC] to His disciples SAYING: All of you accept and eat of HOC: for HOC is My Body.

165

FORCED TO BE PRIEST

The Canonized Latin words--*Qui pridie quam pateretur*...by themselves *force* each priest to stop speaking in the narrative tense and to start acting and speaking *in persona Christi*--in the tense of Christ-priest *agens et dicens* THE DIVINE TRANSFORMATION by his God-empowered *benedixit*. This facet of the perfect Christ-given diamond of infinite worth--the Latin Canonized Mass--can only be destroyed by change.

The First Mass, every Mass, the Eternal Mass (cf. Apoc) and the Bloody Sacrifice of Calvary are each the Saving Will of Christ realized in different ways. At each Mass that Padre Pio and every other validly ordained priest properly says, THE SACRIFICE is realized as these priests *say and do*, not in their own *finite personhood*, but *in the person of Christ*.

The First Mass--actualized at Calvary--is now made present once again. Christ is here. Christ offers Himself for our sins. As the holiest of space-time moments materializes, we utter a thanksgiving to God for priests. *Only* priests *act* or *do* in the person of Christ.

Only priests are Christ made present *into our space-time to effect our salvation in the mystery of faith--the Holy Sacrifice of the Mass. Only* priests celebrate Mass. *Only* priests *suffer into being,* or *realize the oblation,* our only salvation from Hell unto Heaven.

The Lord, *now the Priest in persona Christi, took bread into His holy and venerable hands--* these sacred hands of the Divine Master! In order that priests may perform this same act of the heavenly Lord, their hands were sacramentalized. They were especially anointed, blessed and prayed over by the bishop who ordained them *(at least, in the ordination rites before 1969).*

As their hands were consecrated, their souls were set apart and specially blessed or metamorphasized by God. The words of the Canonized Mass come from Christ. Christ instituted our Mass. Saints and the most ancient tradition assure us that Our Lord, Himself, formulated the Canonized Liturgy.

However, when we compare the words of the liturgical prayer *Qui pridie* with the report of the Last Supper scene, as given us by the Synoptics, do we not find that the words, *into His holy and venerable hands, and with eyes lifted up towards heaven unto Thee, O God, His heavenly Father,* are missing? To this, the Angelic Doctor remarks:

> Our Lord said and did many things which are not written down by the Evangelists; and among them is the uplifting of His eyes to heaven at the supper; nevertheless, the Roman Church had it by tradition from the apostles, who obtained it from Christ. He Who lifted up His eyes to the Father in raising Lazarus to life...in the prayer which He made for the disciples, has more reason to do so in instituting this Sacrament, as being of greater import. (Summa theol., IIIa, q. 83, a.4 ad 2)

Christ--and *the Priest in persona Christi*--lifted up His eyes, giving thanks to God His Almighty

168

Father. He thanked His Heavenly Father that the great moment for the institution of the Sacrifice of the Mass, for which He had so eagerly and lovingly longed during His earthly life, was now at hand. He thanked the Father for willing the salvation of the Elect.

CONSECRATION OR ANNIHILATION OF BREAD

HOC est enim corpus meum.
For HOC is my body.

The Priest's *HOC is My Body* specifies the transubstantiation; that is, the conversion of that which was bread--into *HOC*--into the Body of Christ, the Holy Eucharist. Bread is annihilated. Suddenly, HOC is made present.

> **These words do not make the Body of Christ to be the Body of Christ, nor do they make the bread to be the Body of Christ. Expressly, Our Lord did not say: This bread is My Body, nor this, My Body is My Body, but in**

169

general: HOC is My Body, assigning no noun on the part of the subject, but only a pronoun, which signifies substance in common, without quality, that is, without a determinate form.
(Summa Theol, St. Thomas, II, 3)

After each consecration comes the elevation. Now, those attending Mass adore Christ. They adore *what appears to be bread*--WHO IS REALLY CHRIST. *HOC* is adored, and *HOC* is Christ.

The Priest, in persona Christi, brings Christ, *the Sacrifice for your sins.* Christ, the Holy Eucharist now comes *only as the effect or fruit of THE Unbloody Sacrifice.* Thank Him for The Saving Event. Then, adore *HOC--the Holy Eucharist--* the Fruit given to us through validly functioning priests as they *re-present the Holy Sacrifice.*

St. Thomas also explained *HOC* in another way. *HOC,* which appears to be bread, has the accidents or properties or appearance of bread, but *the substance of HOC is Christ* (Christ without His *accidents* or visible properties). *HOC* is the Effect of *divine transformation* or of transubstantiation.

TRANSUBSTANTIATION occurs.   *Christ's substance replaces the substance which used to underlie the bread.*   HOC looks like bread.   The accidents of bread remain. However, *HOC is truly Christ.* HOC is to be adored since *HOC,* the Holy Eucharist, is Christ.

THE CONSECRATION OF THE WINE

*Simili modo postquam caenatum est, accipiens et hunc praeclarum Calicem in sanctas, ac venerabiles manus suas: item tibi gratias **agens benedixit** deditque discipulis suis, **dicens**: Accipite et bibite ex eo omnes, **hic est enim calix sanguinis mei, novi et aeterni testamenti: mysterium fidei: qui pro vobis et pro multis effundetur in remissionem peccatorum.** Haec quotiescumque feceritis, in mei memoriam facietis.*

*In like manner, after He had supped, taking also into His holy and venerable hands this goodly chalice, likewise **giving** thanks to Thee, He **blessed** it, and gave it to His disciples, **saying**: Take and drink ye of this: **for this is the chalice of my blood, of the new and everlasting testament: the mystery of faith which shall be shed for you and for many unto the remission of sins.** As often as ye shall do these things, do them into My Memoriam.*

When Padre Pio was asked why he suffered so much at the Consecration of the Holy Mass, he answered:

> **You ask me why I suffer. I would like to weep torrents of tears. Don't you comprehend the tremendous mystery?** *God, Victim* **for our sins! And** *priests* **are** *His* **butchers!** (Padre Pio's Mass, Fr. Tarcisio of Cervinara)

In the case of Padre Pio, he was not only *His butcher,* but was himself *butchered,* through, in

Padre Pio Drawing: Barbara Kellam

and into Christ. At the Consecration, Padre Pio, stigmatist-priest, suffered *in persona Christi,* as if he, too were being crucified. *With, through* and *in Christ,* Padre Pio's body was broken so that his blood might be shed, both on his own behalf and for many others.

THE HOLY MASS GOOD FRIDAY

Here is your inspiration or motivation to live *your* Good Friday. Here is *your* Source of graces or powers to live *your* Good Friday, everyday. As we have noted, in Christ's Jewish calendar, our Holy Thursday night *is really* the beginning of Good Friday. Thus, the first Mass and its bloody actualization occurred on the same day--Good Friday. *Pridie* could be understood as *the prime of the day.*

Each Mass brings Good Friday to us. Each Mass repeats the Last Supper. Each Mass brings the Holy Sacrifice--in an unbloody way--into our midst. Each Mass is Christ's Unbloody Sacrifice of Calvary--the heart of Calvary made immediate,

174

so that Christ Himself becomes present to our space and time--Body, Blood, Soul and Divinity, under the appearance of bread and wine. That which appears to be bread or wine *is now Christ Himself.*

Christ's Mass Prayer *is* Christ's Good Friday Saving Will and Testament. This Mass was *suffered into being* or *materialized* in the actual Crucifixion. Here is the heart and the power of your being crucified with Christ. Christ *crucified in you* is your only hope of glory (Col 1:27).

Whenever Christ dwells in any Catholic this side of death, He does so to enact or to complete Good Friday. Each is to be crucified to his own flesh (the natural desires or likings of his own estranged bodily appetites, thinking and desiring) and to his own world--to living for or from anyone other than Christ or Mary who is the only human person *perfectly transparent to God.*

Here, before you, is the Salutary Will, as it were, touched down to enact the Saving-Deed and the Saving-Person at this Mass. Through and in this

Holy Sacrifice and Holy Sacrament, God's Salutary Will may, in like manner, come down upon you and transform you in similar ways--so that the Saving-Deed may be realized in you, as the Saving-Person comes to dwell within you to effect *your* Good Friday crucifixion. It is only through Him, with Him and in Him that you can render eternal positive glory and honor to God for all eternity.

BENEDIXIT: AGENS ET DICENS

From Genesis to the Apocalypse, God *always* encounters man *agens et dicens*--doing and saying in order to BLESS him into salvation from Hell. God BLESSES by doing and speaking.

The Salutary Action and Salutary Person come into our midst at each valid consecration. Then, Christ-priest is *agens* and *dicens* as He BLESSES into being the divine transformation. *GIVING* thanks to His Heavenly father He blessed and gave--*SAYING "This is My Body (or Blood)."*

Only Christ-priest--only he who is validly ordained and thus empowered--may validly BLESS, ACT AND SPEAK *in persona Christi.* Only he *effects* or *makes* CHRIST SO TO ACT AND SPEAK AMONG US AS TO HAVE CHRIST'S SALUTARY ACT AND CONSEQUENTLY CHRIST HIMSELF PRESENT TO THE CHRIST-PRIEST'S SPACE AND TIME--to BLESS into existence: the Saving Deed; the Saving Person *and* the Saved (the Elect).

Only Christ-priests can bless--totally metamorphasize bread and wine--into the Holy Sacrifice and Holy Sacrament. Because Christ has deigned to give us Christ-priests, let us be most grateful and positive.

Without priests, Christ's Salutary Will would have been *realized in space-time only on Good Friday and in Heaven.* As Cardinal Ottaviani and other Catholic theologians have pointed out, *Catholicism does not*--as in heretical and false rites, and as in modern heretical liturgies, *narrate a past event.* By God's power, *Good Friday is re-presented at every valid Mass.*

Catholicism, through its Christ-priests, *makes Christ present among us,* as Vatican Two correctly observed. *Only a Christ-priest in persona Christi,* by his properly *agens et dicens,* is able to *accomplish that which has happened, benedixit* (past tense) the Holy Sacrifice and the Holy Sacrament.

Each Mass *re-presents* God's fulfilment of His initially separating *light* from *darkness* (Gn 1:1-4). In Genesis, the Triune Godhead BLESSED or metamorphasized sin-created chaos into *light* by His ACTING and SPEAKING. So also, in an infinitely greater manner, as the fulfilment of Genesis; and, with *the humility* that only God has, does God now use His designated instrument, a validly functioning priest's BENEDIXIT (to have blessed) or metamorphasized bread and wine into being the Holy Sacrifice and Holy Sacrament by the Christ-priest's properly AGENS (giving thanks) and DICENS (saying).

Here at every valid Mass, the Trinity actualizes or realizes *the Saving Will*--as the Christ-Priest blesses, acts and speaks. Indeed, here is THE MYSTERY OF FAITH--to be adored by the Priest who says Mass and by each of the faithful who are privileged to be present at Mass. As a validly ordained priest validly blesses, acts and speaks, Christ's BROKEN BODY is made present again--*re-presented;* and, Christ's SHED BLOOD comes to save the Elect.

Christ's BODY (not that which *was* bread) comes into being as BROKEN so that His BLOOD may be shed; and, so that the faithful may be able to eat THIS BODY and, as it were, thus assimilate IT. Only *in this manner,* can the Elect live--*no longer them, BUT Christ in them* (Ga 2:20; Php 1:21). Likewise, Christ's BLOOD comes to us as *SHED for the forgiveness of the sins of God's Elect ones* (Php 1:21) through their drinking IT.

KNOWN AND PRAYED BY PADRE PIO

In the liturgy of the Canon, we find preserved the

very same order of the words describing the sequence of Christ's actions, as given by the three Synoptics: *giving thanks, blessed* and *saying.* St. Thomas calls attention to the fact that *blessed,* together with the participles *giving thanks* and *saying* connect the words spoken by Christ simultaneous with His action, for he says:

> It is not necessary for the sequence to be understood only with respect to the last word spoken, as if Christ had just then pronounced those words when He gave it to His disciple; but the sequence can be understood with regard to all that had gone before...thus...all of the pertinent consecration prayers define the Mass.
> (Summa Theologica, St. Thomas, IIIa, q. 78).

Writing on the Mass, Cardinal Saint John Newman states:

> To me, nothing is so consoling, so piercing, so thrilling, so overcoming, as the Holy Mass, said as it is among us. I could attend Masses forever and not be tired. It is not a mere form of words. It

is a great action, THE GREATEST ACTION THAT CAN BE ON EARTH. It is not the invocation merely, but, if I dare to use the word, the EVOCATION of the Eternal.

He becomes present on the altar in flesh and blood before Whom the angels bow and devils tremble. Here is that awful event which is the scope and the interpretation of every part of the solemnity.

Words are necessary, but as means, not as ends. They are not mere addresses to the throne of grace. They are instruments of what is far higher, of consecration, of sacrifice. (St. John Newman)

And Padre Pio tells us:

How happy Jesus makes me! How sweet is His spirit! I am confused. I do nothing but weep. What distresses me is that I repay all this love from Jesus with so much ingratitude. (Padre Pio)

181

MORE ON BENEDIXIT AGENS AND DICENS

Perhaps no greater insight into the Mass can be given than the pristine biblical one. Far surpassing what good authors do, God, in the beginning of His Bible, summarized not only the Bible, but the *now-present* and eternity itself--not only for mankind *but also* for each individual.

The first four verses of God's Bible give each of us a summary of his own life. Each is born within the *awlah tohu-bohu*--the cursed and desolate darkness or in a *God-cursed state*. Somehow, each is given a chance to embrace *the Salutary Light* (cf. Jn 1). Finally and forever, the *dark* kingdom will be separated from the kingdom of *light*. Hell will be forever separate from Heaven.

On whatever side one finds himself at the final moment of death determines where he will spend eternity. Let's meditate on these first verses that God gave to us men who dwell in the darkness of sin (all of us, except, of course, Our Lady).

In the beginning God made whatever began. CURSED AND DESOLATE BLESSED with the Holy Ghost ACTING and the Son SPEAKING--'LET LIGHT BE.' LIGHT WAS and it was good. God separated light from darkness (Gn 1:1-4--*according to the original Hebrew Bible*).

In Adam, God created the human family. No sooner had God created, *sin* messed up God's creation. Cursed and desolate darkness results-- *awlah tohu-bohu.*

Then, God the Father salutarily wills or BLESSES His Elect into being. He saves them from Hell. "The Holy Ghost [is] ACTING and the Son SPEAKING."

These words--ACTING (AGENS), BLESSED (BENEDIXIT) and SPEAKING (DICENS)--are the key words ushering in SALVATION from naturally inevitable darkness--eternal Hell. These key words appear in each of the accounts of the First Mass as given to us by the Synoptics. These key words appear in the Canonized Mass. Are not the priest's utterance of these key words essential for a valid Mass?

"God separated the light from the darkness (Gn 1:3)." For all eternity, the *sin-mess*--the evil and cursed darkness--will be separated from God-blessed and God-endowed *Light*. This is accomplished by God's salutary Will--by the Holy Sacrifice.

According to God's Bible and the testimony of classical saints, *few* (very few) find the narrow door; and then, walk the narrow path which alone can save them from their natural fate. *Most* fail to conquer the *sin-mess*. *Most* become temporal and eternal *victims* of and in the *sin-mess*. *Most* will be eternally damned by God.

Few positively respond to God's BLESSING, ACTING and SPEAKING light or salvation in order *to destroy* darkness or damnation. This BLESSING, ACTING and SPEAKING is to be found in God's Greatest Gift--each valid Mass. How can we escape *if* we neglect--or worse yet, distort or reject--*so great salvation* (Heb 2:3)?

184

ORDAINED TO CONSECRATE OR TO BLESS BY ACTING AND SAYING

As at Padre Pio's ordination, so also was it at mine. When I was ordained a Jesuit priest in 1966, I was ordained not in a vague sense to celebrate the Holy Sacrifice of the Mass; but specifically *to salutarily consecrate and to bless.* Thus, did I receive the almighty power of God Himself to *salutarily bless*--to bless God's Greatest Gift into *here and now* existence.

As at Padre Pio's ordination, so also at my ordination ceremony, I received the imposition of the Archbishop's hands and of the hands of many priests. And after being clothed by the Archbishop in the priestly vestments, each in turn, we knelt before him as he sat on a chair with the white gremial veil on his lap. I extended towards him the palms of my hands, which he anointed with the consecrated Oil of Catechumens, while reciting this beautiful, inspiring and powerful prayer (which was eliminated in the 1969 revision):

*Consecrare et sanctificare digneris,
Domine, manus istas per istam
unctionem et nostram benedictionem.
Amen. Ut quaecumque benedixerint,
benedicantur, et quaecumque
consecraverint, consecrentur et
sanctificentur, in nomine Domini nostri
Jesu Christi. Amen.*

*Deign, O Lord, to CONSECRATE AND
MAKE HOLY these hands by this
unction and our BLESSING. Amen. So
that what they will BLESS will be
BLESSED; what they will
CONSECRATE will be CONSECRATED
AND MADE HOLY in the name of our
Lord Jesus Christ. Amen.*

Padre Pio and I were validly ordained priests.
Through Christ, we were specifically given the
God-power (of the Father) to *salutarily bless*--to
totally metamorphasize or to destroy and
salutarily recreate. We can *bless* bread and wine
so as to destroy them, and in their place to make
present Christ's Holy Sacrifice and Christ
Himself--Body, Blood, Soul and Divinity. What

God-awesome power! This is awesome not only for priests, but also for those who are privileged to attend. This is awesome for those who (through, *in and into* this *blessing*) die to being Hell-bent sinners in order to become the Elect.

CHAPTER SEVENTEEN

HIS BODY BROKEN HIS BLOOD SHED

"During the celebration of Mass, at what moment do you suffer the most?"

"From the Consecration to Communion."
(Padre Pio, Padre Pio's Mass, Fr. Tarcisio of Cervinara, p. 35)

In each Holy Mass, the Body and Blood of His eternally Beloved Son is offered up to the Heavenly Father. (The Holy Sacrifice of the Mass, Gihr, p.662)

"Caro cibus, sanguis potus"--taken from the Lauda Sion sequence of the Feast of Corpus Christi. *His Body Broken to be our food. His Blood shed to be our drink.*

He *blessed*--totally metamorphasized bread in accord with His Will; broke [His Body] and gave to His apostles saying: take and eat *HOC. Hoc* is My [broken] Body.

His Body is broken! His Blood is shed! Why?

The Saving Deed is accomplished in order to let His Body and His Blood be assimilated by certain sinners unto their salvation from Hell--for forgiveness of the sins of a select group of people. At each Mass, the Elect (past, present and future) are *effected into being.*

The adored Body of Christ contained His adored Blood. How could this Blood become redemptive? In God's Providence, His Blood had to be shed and drunk in a proper manner or with the correct salutary attitude (I Cor 11). For His Blood to be thus shed, Christ's Body had to be broken. *"Caro cibus..."* for His Body to become food to be *eaten,* Christ's Body had to be broken.

Unless one eats Christ's Body and drinks His Blood, he cannot be saved (Jn 6:53). This is Redemption *as revealed.* This is Reality directed toward us. Here is salvation *as determined by God.*

"Sanguis potus..." In God's Providence, the adored Body must be broken. The Vessel must be broken so that His Blood may flow and be drunk

unto salvation by His Elect.

Christ is God made a man so that God may give His all. In Christ, God gave His all. God gave Himself--Body and Blood. No wonder Padre Pio referred to priests as *butchers of Christ* and thus *butchers of God* (since Christ is God).

God does all things to ultimate and unimaginable perfection. His Greatest Gift is thus given to His Elect. Any proper understanding of this Gift which may be given to you will never exhaust Reality. What are we to do with Christ's broken Body and His shed Blood? We are to eat and drink unto salvation from Hell.

Eat. Assimilate and become like unto Christ. In and through Christ, each of the Elect's body is to become like unto Christ's Body--broken in conformity to God's Salutary Will.

Drink. Let Christ's shed Blood become your life-force. Live no longer you, but Christ in you. Live with the *mind and heart* of Christ.

Imitating Christ, shed your blood--Christ's Blood in you. Imitate Padre Pio as best you can. At least, take to heart what was manifested in the stigmatist-priest's death: Padre Pio's blood was shed to its last drop; at his death, his stigmatic wounds dried up; a transparent layer of skin covered the totally drained wounds, as noted previously.

CHAPTER EIGHTEEN

CHRIST'S LAST WILL AND TESTAMENT

Every Holy Mass heard with devotion produces in our hearts marvelous effects. (Padre Pio).

St. Augustine, reflecting Catholic teaching, assures us that God will judge each justly. However, His Saving Mercy will not be extended to all. Those who go to Hell forever, will justly go. Those who go to Heaven will be the recipients of God's freely bestowed saving Mercy. God is in charge, not man.

Jesus didn't leave us with any earthly goods when He made out His Last Will and Testament--the New and Eternal Testament in His Blood. He left us a *morasha*--the Jewish word for a specific type of inheritance. *Hic est enim calix Sanguinis Mei novi et aeterni testamenti mysterium fidei.* Christ left us the *morasha--the Chalice of His Blood,* the Mystery of Faith.

JEWISH ROOTS

From earliest times, God left His special people, the Jewish people, three different benefices--the Torah, the land of Israel and life eternal. At the Last Supper, Jesus primarily leaves life eternal--a*eterni Testamenti, Mysterium Fidei.*

The *morasha* is the new and eternal Last Will and Testament of Jesus. It is the Mystery of Faith. This *morasha* has the same basic elements common to the other two *morasha.*

AN OPPORTUNITY

First of all, a *morasha* is not a *yerusha*--an outright gift, such as a piece of property. *A morasha* **is** *a real opportunity*--**something that must be worked in order to become profitable to the recipient or beneficiary.** The Mystery of Faith must be perceived and properly *acted upon.*

Padre Pio and I were both left the same Gift--the Canonized Mass. Padre Pio worked his Gift far more than I have.

The heresy of *once saved, always saved* would be a *yerusha*. Christ left a *morasha*--work out your salvation diligently (Phlp 2:12). Christ did not leave a *yerusha*.

Just how diligently must you work? **"This is the Chalice of Blood, drink of it."** The pearl of great price can be attained only by Blood (sweat and tears)--your willingness to drink, assimilate and make your own the *shed blood* of Christ. Agonize to walk the road to eternal life, as Scripture in the Greek original clearly states. Faith, without such works, is not only dead, but also detrimental unto eternal salvation.

Remember the action word. *Agonize!* Agonize by shedding your blood, uniting your heroic efforts to Christ's shed Blood. That's the Mass. That's how you can participate in the Mass, the Mystery of Faith, if you are graced to do so, of course. That's your *morasha*--your *opportunity*!

Jewish sages connect *morasha* with its cognate

"*m'orashi*"--a beloved fiancee. Should not each Catholic be a fiancee to Christ? Is not each *engaged to* Christ? What is the *first* and most important commandment? Should not each love Christ courageously, sacrificially and exclusively? Should not each love Christ as a true *m'orasahi* loves--fiercely?

A WAY OF LIFE

The third and last meaning of a *morasha* is a way of life. When they die, successful parents leave behind children formed with certain outstanding virtues. They leave behind living legacies of specific virtues--children who live as they were taught or, at least, were taught how to live as they should.

Christ left behind both the Old and New Testaments. These show us how to live in order to attain our eternal benefice, our *morasha*--the eternal Testament of Christ's love. The Bible tells us how to live. We are to live, not us, but Christ in us (1Co 9:14). Christ's Bible and Apostolic

Tradition give us the once and forever Christ-bestowed faith and morals (social and liturgical) which we are to believe or do in order to be saved from eternal Hell. Here is the Christ-given *new and eternal covenant*--waiting for you to ratify or make your own by what you say and do, as it were, the covenant in Christ's Blood with your own *"Christ-ed"* blood.

SHED YOUR BLOOD

The eternal jewels of Christ are those from which His Blood was shed for your redemption. He left you *morasha*, not a *yerusha*. You, too, must live shedding your blood united to the Chalice of His shed Blood. Only thus can you be an heir of Christ. Only those who are united to Christ-crucified will be united to Christ-glorified. That's the meaning of Christ's *morasha*, His Last Will and Testament in His shed Blood, the Mystery of Faith, the Holy Sacrifice of the Mass.

With Padre Pio as model and inspiration, shed your blood. Come to live, not you, but Christ in you--Christ to be crucified in you. Shed--not your life-blood--but your life-blood transformed or blessed by Christ's Blood. As it were, have your blood *blessed* into becoming Christ's Blood in you--His life-force--so that you may be so united with Christ-crucified unto the shedding of His Blood (which was your blood, transformed by Christ)--for the eternal salvation of your soul and for the eternal salvation of other souls (because of the God-given Colossians' mystery, which we have already considered).

CHAPTER NINETEEN

ANAPHORA

By means of the unbloody immolation (in the August Sacrifice of the Altar) the High Priest (Jesus Christ) continues to do that which He already did on the Cross by offering Himself to the Eternal Father as the only and most acceptable Victim. (Mediator Dei, Pope Pius XII, 1947)

HOC is My Body; this is the Chalice of My blood. Take; eat; drink. Always theologians ask questions such as the following. *How is this possible? How does this happen? What, exactly, does happen in this transformation? What is the cause?* No answer seems to be satisfactory.

Which words are needed? Which are superfluous? Why ask? Does not our very asking tend to *destroy* the sacred? Does not our very asking in most cases betray evil, or even sacrilegious, intent? Why else purpose to change the canonized words of the Canonized Liturgy?

Substance, accidents? One immediately senses that something is lacking by the way *man theorizes Mystery*. Also, something is awesomely wrong when men reduce the Holy Sacrifice, the Mystery of Faith, to the categories of time, substance and causality, *the very categories of this world*. How dare we treat mystery--*the Mystery*--as an object of our critical inquiries? How dare we be so irreverent to the Most Holy?

Also something is lacking when theologians focus on words, *forgetting the totality and ignoring the mystery of the whole liturgy*. When theologians give a definition to the Most Holy, they raise more questions than they answer. Then, as they attempt to answer the new questions--again, they create ever more problems.

Let well enough be. Let the very best be. Don't question the Most Holy in order to modify it. Always, treat with utmost respect *the Christ-given form (or words of the Mass) which we have received from Apostolic Tradition*. Refrain from judging, especially judging so as to modify. Study and learn in a positive way, so as to come to a greater appreciation of the *incarnation of God's Saving Will, given to us by Christ Jesus.*

THE CANONIZED LITURGY'S ANAPHORA

The whole liturgy reflects the *incarnation of* and the *participation in God's Saving Will.* The Canonized Mass effects the anaphora or the ascending movement.

The very goal of this movement of ascension *is to take us out of being victims of our flesh and of the community, this world,* and to make us partakers of Heavenly mystery, the Mystery of Faith. The Mystery of Faith *uswards (in order to enrich our lowly position)* is our being placed on the paten in order to be blessed or metamorphasized through, in and into Christ. The Mystery of Faith is not to be banally proclaimed, but rather the awesome Mystery of Faith is to be adored, partaken of and loved.

Oblation--Christ, being crucified in you--in your dying to the flesh and to the world--is the anaphora, *the lifting up of your soul out of flesh and world.* This anaphora is possible only through the Mass. This anaphora is the Mass. *Lift up your hearts.* Is your response as follows?

> *I lift my heart to God, to be crucified through, in and into Christ, to my flesh and to the world. Let the Saving Will be realized in me, as I eat His Body and drink His Blood. May the Saving Will elevate me into God's Kingdom. May the Saving Will lead me to positively glorify God, now and forever. Amen.*

Do this into My Memory is primarily the commission given by Christ to His chosen few-- validly ordained priests. What an awesome commission! We dare not fail to do *exactly as Christ decreed to us through Apostolic Tradition.*

Do into My Memory also applies, in a secondary and transferred sense, to each of Christ's Elect souls. Each of the Elect, de facto, *does his life* and *has his life done into the Memory of Christ.* The Memory comes into our here and now to bring us up into the infinite and eternal. As it were, as the bread is annihilated by God's BLESSING through His priest, so also must each of us join the Holy Eucharist on the paten by being annihilated and living Christ Crucified.

"Blessed is the Kingdom of the Father, Son and Holy Ghost." So begins Mass. Mass is that Kingdom which beams us up to Heaven, even as it comes down to us in space-time.

Somehow, Mass worship is no longer bound to time, but brings us out of time into eternity. It does not have to keep days and hours. It is always in God's eternal Kingdom. When we worship, we step out of time. Somehow, the Elect worship God in Truth and in Spirit--in the Heavenly life.

On earth, the Elect celebrate feasts with an attitude or purpose which connects Christ's life with nature's times and seasons. Only in this way can we poor mortals come to possess ever deepening convictions about the Saving Deed and the Saving Person. Only in this way can the time-imprisoned redeem time as they focus on those moments in time through which they can be redeemed.

The liturgical cycle, as well as each Rosary, remind us of the dimension of salvation. Padre Pio, the mystic priest was blessed to live the whole liturgical cycle, especially, that which pertained to the suffering of Christ. His favorite mysteries were the sorrowful mysteries.

GOD'S SALUTARY POWER AND PRESENCE

When God blesses, inevitably His Will is done on earth or in Heaven. God the Father BLESSED-- He (transubstantiated) willed and thus brought into being: the destruction of bread and wine into the Body and Blood of His Son at each *valid* Mass (that was, is and will be said) from the Last Supper to the last Mass on earth. Thus, He BLESSED into being *the multis*--each of the Elect. All of this He *did, does and will do* through Christ the Son *speaking* and the Holy Ghost *(agens) doing,* or *(gratias agens) giving graces.*

The Father's Will, Christ's Salutary Action, is accomplished in the power of the Holy Ghost, Who does or acts *doing graces (gratias agens)* at the Consecration of every valid Mass. For all of this, we strive to be most thankful. We strive to be EUCHARISTIC. St. Leonard of Port Maurice tells us:

> Behold the heavenly rainbow, pacifying the storms of Divine Justice! For myself, I believe that, were it not for the Holy Mass, at this present moment, the world would be in the abyss, unable to bear up under the mighty load of its iniquities. (St. Leonard of Port Maurice)

It is most fitting to now recall the Mass-prayer which was given by the angel to the little children of Fatima in 1916:

> **O MOST HOLY TRINITY, Father, Son and Holy Ghost, I adore Thee profoundly. I offer Thee the Most Precious Body, Blood, Soul and Divinity of Our Lord and Saviour, Jesus Christ, present in all the**

tabernacles throughout the world, in reparation for the outrages, sacrileges and indifferences by which He Himself is offended. By the infinite merits of His Most Sacred Heart and the intercession of the Immaculate Heart of Mary, I beg for the conversion of poor sinners.

Indeed, the Canonized Eastern Liturgy edifies us by emphasizing that *Christ alone pleases God and that to please God, we must unite our minds and hearts in obedience to Christ.*

Holy to the Holiest. One is Holy; One is Lord--Jesus Christ, to the glory of God the Father, forever and ever. Amen.

CHAPTER TWENTY

MYSTERIUM FIDEI

The Victim is one and the same, the same now offering by the ministry of the priest, who once offered Himself on the Cross, the manner of offering alone being different.(The dogmaticCouncil of Trent)

The Sacrifice of the Mass is really the holy and living representation and at the same time, the bloodless and efficacious offering of the passion of the Lord and of that Sacrifice in Blood which was offered for us on the Cross. (Opus Catechisticum de sacramentis, St. Peter Canisius, q. 7)

All internal heretics despise the Holy Sacrifice *as instituted by Christ.* They believe in the Holy Sacrifice *past tense--in the past and over with.* As the greatest theologian of the twentieth century, Cardinal Ottaviani, observed:

Such heretics logically reduce the Consecration prayers to the *past and over with tense* or *to a mere narrative.*(The Critical Study of Novus Ordo Missae, 1969)

Along with other significant words, *Mystery of Faith* uttered by the priest within *his* consecratory prayers both *effect* and *proclaim essential Catholicism*--**the presence of the Body and Blood of Christ in Sacrifice and Sacrament, within the Christ-priest's here and now. Christ-priest brings into being THE MYSTERY OF FAITH for us to *adore*--not to proclaim aloud. Be silent. Adore!**

As it were, when one distills the Blood out of the Bloody Sacrifice on Calvary, what remains? *One Sacrifice, different manners of offering-- bloody or unbloody.* So *defines* the Church. This same Sacrifice is each valid Mass. Here, the Mystery of Faith is realized among us. *Adore,* where our adoration is insufficient. Adore, *where not to adore,* would be sinful. Adore God bringing the Saving Deed and (thus) the Saving Person of Good Friday into our here and now.

The Day of Salvation is Good Friday, the Day

which begins with the first Mass on *our Holy Thursday eve* and ends with Christ entombed. At each Canonized Mass, Good Friday is liturgized and applied in time and space. For all of Heaven's eternity, Good Friday is liturgized, fully revealed and adored (Apoc 5:12). At each valid Mass in space-time, Good Friday is liturgized and revealed by faith to be adored. Here is the Mystery of Faith.

Before Christ came as Saviour, God commanded anticipatory (yet) deficient sacrifices like those of Melchisedech, Abraham and Abel. These sacrifices were acceptable by virtue of the Holy Sacrifice. To prove this, on the day that the Mystery of Faith was first actualized, the tombs of these saints were opened and these saints were seen in the Holy City (Mt 27:53), even as their souls were being loosed from the hold of Limbo.

The Holy Sacrifice was uniquely liturgized and then *actualized in Christ's Blood* on that great day, Good Friday: *"His broken Body, our only food. His dripping Blood our only drink. Because of which we call this Friday Good."*

EFFECTIVE SACRIFICE

The dogmatic Councils of Trent and Florence defined the Mass, the Holy Sacrifice, as the *efficacious* or *effective Salutary Action.* The Holy Sacrifice brings about actual salvation. The Holy Sacrifice brings about the actual salvation of *multis--only the Elect.* It is the very essence of salvation and the Heart of Heaven. Good Friday, each Mass, the Heart of Heaven--accomplishes and accomplished salvation for the Elect and only for the Elect. This is Church Dogma.

CHRIST'S WILL

We are not dealing here with man's will. We are considering God's Will--the Will of Christ as given to and as defining, His Church. Christ is *"the same now offering...Who once offered Himself on the Cross, the manner of offering alone being different.*(The Dogmatic First Council of Trent) The Mystery of Faith is equally Good Friday (as explained), each Mass and the Eternal Mass (Rev 5).

As St. Peter Canisius observed, at each Mass the Holy Sacrifice is re-presented, (or made present again) in an unbloody manner, in as much as God can do so and in an effective way--only for the Elect. Only as totally effective can each Mass be what it is--the Heart of Heaven (Rev 5). What an infinitely good and beautiful treasure Jesus has entrusted to His Church--the very Heart of Heaven! Who dares modify and thus, sacrilege, Christ's most precious gift--the Canonized Mass?

Rest content with the Mass as defined by Christ and as canonized by His Church. Refuse to pervert the Mass so as to accomodate and express the currently popular mega-sin of presumption. Whether you like it or not, the Mass effects salvation only for the Elect. All are not saved. Only the Elect are saved; and unless you have had a very special revelation from God, you cannot claim to be certainly one of the Elect without becoming one of the damned (so dogmatizes the Council of Trent).

Accept the Mass as instituted by Christ and as canonized by His Church. Accept and be positive.

Make the sign of your election--for example, your coming to a true notion of the Mass--*sure.* Actualize the sign of your salvation. With Padre Pio as an example, come to pray and live the Mass so as to be united with Christ now as Crucified and forever as Glorified.

CHAPTER TWENTY-ONE

ENTER THE DIVINE PRESENT

My God, I believe, I adore, I hope, I love Thee. I ask pardon for those who do not believe, nor adore, nor hope, nor love Thee.

Most Holy Trinity, Father, Son and Holy Ghost, I adore Thee profoundly. I offer Thee the Most Precious Body, Blood, Soul and Divinity of Thy Most Beloved Son, Our Lord and Saviour, Jesus Christ, present in all the tabernacles throughout the world, in reparation for all the outrages, sacrileges and indifferences by which He Himself is offended.

And through the infinite merits of His Most Sacred Heart and the intercession of the Immaculate Heart of Mary, I pray for the conversion of poor sinners.
(The Eucharistic Prayers from Fatima).

A validly ordained priest, properly saying the

Christ-ordained Canonized Mass, effects a remembrance charged with such reality that it *materializes the Saving Action--past, present and eternal.* God the Father's *benedixit* or salvation from Hell, is made present through the Holy Ghost *agens* and the Son *dicens* (Gn 1). Thus, does God the Father *bless* or *do*--as often as His priests do. God the Father *Will-ing* to *bless,* God the Son *dicens;* and God the Holy Ghost *agens*--such Divine activity now and eternally *re-creates* or redeems. (This is the fulfillment or full explanation of the Divine activity as described in Genesis and as previously explained).

We are here at Mass--to fear, to wonder and to adore. Each of the Elect is glad that he cannot grasp the depths of God's being by his reason. He is filled with a holy wonder. He is filled with terror before God--that terror of which the Old Testament speaks so often, a fear which is born even from the faintest awareness of God, especially of God *benedixit, agens* and *dicens* salvation into our here and now; and, ecstatically, into Heaven forever and ever.

Each of the Elect lives two lives in this world. By his body which will die, *he is of the earth.* With his spirit, *he lives in the Divine Present.*

The Mystery of Faith, God's gift of acceptable worship, makes it possible for each of the Elect to transcend this miserable and wretched world and to participate in the world which is God's, the world of the Divine Presence--the world of the Divine Present.

THROUGH CHRIST THE ELECT ARE HERE AND IN HEAVEN

Each of the Elect somehow lives on earth and in Heaven. Each of the Elect somehow *realizes* Heaven at each Mass even as he is *realized into Heaven* by and at each Mass.

Even while on earth, the Elect already stand in God's everlasting today and take part in the *action of Heaven's life.* Padre Pio, even from his earliest childhood, lived *in the Heavens,* as he communed not only with Christ and Mary but with the saints in Heaven. However, for the rest of us, Heavenly realities can only be seen (and not realized) in shadows perceived by Faith.

The Father gives the whole of Life to the Son, in agape--Divine Love. The Son gives Himself back to the Father. The Father and the Son breathe forth the Holy Ghost to one another. This exchange of Life is the work of eternity and constitutes infinite and eternal Life within the Trinity.

It is into this Life and work that we are taken by *the Mystery.* For God's love, His agape, willed to give itself to some of us. This love re-created or redeemed some sin-cursed humans in order to make them partakers of His divinity. The Son redeemed the Elect. Through the Son made Man, the Holy Ghost sanctifies the Elect through the Mass.For this reason, the Church has *dogmatized: extra ecclesiam, nulla salus (outside the Church, there is no salvation).*

Christ now lives on earth in His Elect, as it were, to *crucify them into Heaven.* He lives to *oblate* each of His elect--to make each Christ-ed soul into His Memory by being made conformable to His Memory, that is, Christ's suffering and dying in obedience to God out of love for God to redeem sinners.

CHAPTER TWENTY-TWO

IN MEMORIAM

From the sacristy, it was a short distance to the Altar. I would say a walk of two, three minutes. But in that time, you would see Padre Pio change completely. It was as if he really were carrying a cross as he approached the Altar. (Fr. Joseph Alessio)

Padre Pio, who had appeared robust only a half-hour before, now shuffled along, his feet wounded, his shoulders weighted. His hands moved gingerly, as though it hurt even to make a motion with them.

At the Consecration, Calvary's meaning became starker. Blood flowed freely from his palms, as if nails had just been driven through them. (CATHOLIC DIGEST, *They Knew Padre Pio*, Kathleen Stauffer, 12/91)

Mysterium Fidei qui pro vobis et pro multis effundetur in remissionem peccatorum...Haec quotiescumque feceritis in mei memoriam facietis.

Here is the Mystery of Faith. Christ's Blood shed to save certain sinners from Hell. As often as you do these and all other things in the same spirit with the graces obtained from Mass--Christ in you will accomplish them into His Memory.

What has just happened? The Heart of Heaven has reversed the life of sin, for the Elect--for those who do or act *into* the Memoriam of Christ. Here is the Source, Sustenance and infinite Summit of any and all of their worthwhile deeds. Here is The Mystery of Faith.

Remember, you remain forever as defined by your earth-memories. This side of death, you are fabricating or defining *you*. You are making your eternal memory--the only personal thing that persists and defines you after your inevitable death. Will this *you*, defined by your memories, be worthless trash that must be forever burned in the horrible fires of Hell?

Will you, as defined by your memories, be of infinite worth? If so, it is because somehow, Christ Crucified came to you and lived in you to transform your worthless memories into His Memoriam of infinite worth. *Facite in Memoriam Meam!* Do into My Memory!

Here is how it all occurs. Here is where it all occurs. Here is the Heart of Heaven brought into our space and time. Here is the Prayer, the Sacrifice--*that only which makes holy (sacrum-facet) or sacri-fices.* Here is the Mystery of Faith--Christ's Blood shed, saving sinners from Hell. Here, one obtains the grace of perseverance.

Adore or be damned. Christ's Sacrifice is the only Way for your memories not to damn you to awesomely painful eternal burning. The Mystery of Faith creates the Elect--those sinners who are saved from Hell.

ADAM'S CURSE

*O felix culpa...*O happy fall of Adam, the head of

humanity. It led to the infinite worth--the incorporation of the Elect into Christ forever within the Godhead. O happy fall! O happy fall for the chosen few. For those who will not be saved, some of the saddest words of the Bible are: *"Eve told Adam: 'Take and eat.' He took and he ate (Gn 3)."*

Adam, the federal head of humanity, disobeyed God. By this one sin, Adam shut out Heaven for himself and for all of his progeny. Indeed, he was the federal head of the human race--the father and mother (Eve came from Adam) of every other human being. As such, Adam represented you and me. Somehow, his sin was our sin--our *original* sin.

Jesus is the one and only Saviour. He saves as He wills--not as man decides. His actual saving--His creation and sustenance of the Elect--is the Mystery of Faith. How can you escape eternal damnation if you neglect or fail to properly respond to *so great salvation* (Hb 2:3) the Holy *Sacrifice* in our very midst? Unless you eat the flesh of the Son of Man and drink His blood, you shall not be saved from your *naturally inevitable* Hell (cf. Jn 6:31-58). So wills the Saviour. So must you do--if at all possible, of course--or be damned to Hell.

He blessed the bread, thus metamorphasizing bread into His Body. He broke His Body and gave It to His disciples: Take. Eat. This is My Body, broken for your sins. Thus, did He give these free moral agents the grace or *potency* to have eternal life* (Jn 6:53).

Finally, sin's dark curse of inevitable Hell, as separation from the God Life with or without infinitely horrible pain, is lifted and reversed. The Elect of God dare not question, doubt, reject or *change and thus make sacrilege of* this Christ-Gift, the Mystery of Faith, coming to us from Christ through Apostolic Tradition, through the properly said words in valid Masses of the Canonized Liturgy. The Elect will love Him. They will obey Him fully. They will cherish and preserve liturgical Apostolic Tradition. They will cherish and preserve intact the Holy Sacrifice of the Mass.

Be positive to your one and only prayer--your one and only Way to avoid Hell. Obey or be damned.

FEW ARE SAVED

He, Adam, ate and received the chalice of suffering--a cursed matrix within which to make his memory eternal. This chalice he passed on to his progeny. Therefore, *many* go to Hell:

Many go to Hell. (Jesus)
Many go to Hell. (Our Lady)
Many go to Hell. (all of the saints)

Therefore, (as the original Greek accurately insists) *agonize* to find the Way to avoid naturally inevitable Hell. *Agonize* to follow that path. Jesus demands this! Agonize! Only a few will be saved from eternal Hell. Agonize to be one of the few!

Take this all of you. Drink from this.
This is the chalice of My Blood--the
Chalice of Agony--which will be shed
for you and for the multitude who will be
saved from Hell.

This is the Mystery of Faith--Christ's *effective* Salutary Deed. *This* is to be your life--Christ shedding His Blood. Drink. Let this alone be your Life-blood--you, *suffering through* and *into* Christ for your salvation from Hell and for the salvation of others from Hell. This is your life-- the Holy Sacrifice of Mass. Take this Chalice. Accept and *do* Christ's sufferings in you for the salvation of yourself and other sinners from Hell.

This Mass was and remains the life of Padre Pio. He said and lived the Canonized Mass to such an extent that God rewarded him with a unique blessing. He became the first stigmatist-priest in the Church's history, as he saved souls from Hell through living the Mystery of Faith. In a manner like unto Padre Pio, you should likewise be positive to the Mystery of Faith, the Heart of Heaven, the Holy Sacrifice of the Mass, the Memoria, the Prayer, and the Oblation. Let it be done in you into the eternal Memoria of Christ.

Mysterium Fidei--the Mystery of Faith--Christ and His Saving Event or Saving Deed constitute the essence of The Mystery of Faith. Christ's

Saving Event comes to us at each valid Mass by a Christ-priest--a validly ordained and validly functioning priest who speaks and does *in persona Christi,* in the person of Christ Himself. Out of and within this unique Saving Event, comes Christ, the Holy Eucharist. Here is the essence of The Mystery of Faith--not to be publicly proclaimed or validated but to be personally adored and prayerfully applied to each of our lives. We pray and work so as to be part of The Mystery of Faith.

Let us proclaim silently: *"MY LORD AND MY GOD!"* as HOC, the Sacred Hostia (Victim), and the Chalice are elevated by the Christ-Priest at the Consecration of the Mass. This Memoria of Christ (The Holy Sacrifice) saved the Elect. Heaven, for all Elect rational creatures (angels and men) is for all eternity praising the slain Lamb.

> *Worthy is the Lamb Who was slain, to receive all power, honor, glory, adoration, praise and blessings. Amen.*
> *(Apoc 5:12, 14)*

CHAPTER TWENTY-THREE

UNDE MEMORES

Padre Pio's Mass lasted three hours. People stood wide-eyed. They wept.
(Padre Pio, Oscar De Liso, 1960)

UNDE ET MEMORES, Domine, nos servi tui, sed et plebs tua sancta, ejusdem Christi Filii tui, Domini nostri tam beatae Passionis, nec non et ab inferis Resurrectionis, sed et in coelos gloriosae Ascensionis: offerimus praeclarae majestati tuae de tuis donis ac datis, hostiam puram, hostiam sanctam, hostiam immaculatam, Panem sanctum vitae aeternae, et Calicem salutis perpetuae.

*THUS, through the Mystery of Faith done into **the Memory**, are we, Thy abject slaves, Thy Holy People, saved from Hell (unde) and made into **memores** of the same Jesus Christ Our Lord, Thy Son. We, Thy Holy People, are taken into Christ's Passion, into His*

225

*Resurrection from the realm of death;
and into His glorious Ascension into
Heaven. We offer to Thy Divine Majesty
(of, from and because of)* **the once given
and the continually being given: the
pure Victim; the sanctifying Victim; the
sin-conquering Victim--the Holy
Bread: the Source, Sustenance and
Summit of eternal life and the Chalice
of our perpetually being saved from
Hell and unto Heaven.**

*Unde et memores, Domine, nos servi tui, sed et
plebs tua sancta.* Born from, or out of damnation,
part of and within this Mystery of Faith, are the
Elect, the Memores. These Elect are *nos servi tui-
-*we who join Mary and become abject slaves of
God. *Behold the abject female slave of God, be it
done to me--and then by me--according to Thy
Will.* (Lu 1:38)

Plebs tua sancta comprise the totality of these
Elect who are *born from, part of and within this*
Mystery of Faith. From whence come these
memores, the Elect--who are born from, part of
and within this Mystery of Faith? *Ejusdem*

Christi Filii Tui Domini nostri tam Passionis.
The *memores* are of Christ the Son, Our Lord,
most emphatically (tam) *of His Passion.*

Where is this vast body of all of the *memores,* the
Elect?   *Ejusdem...nec non et ab inferis
Resurrectionis, sed et in caelos gloriosae
Ascensionis.* As saints in Heaven, they are *into
their own heavens of Christ's Resurrection and
thus His resurrecting sinners from Hell (ab inferi)
and Christ's glorious Ascension.* They are in
caelos gloriosae Ascensionis. They are *in caelos-*
-in the Heaven of Christ Glorified.

The saints on earth and in Purgatory are of Christ,
the One and only Saviour Who saves only those
who obey Him and His Revelations, but they do
not have this full realization, as do the saints in
Heaven. The *memores* on earth are of the Risen
and Eternally Glorified Christ, who is each
person's one and only possible link into Heaven
and salvation from Hell.

What do all of the *memores* or saints now do?
Offerimus praeclarae majestati tuae de tuis donis

*ac datis...*we offer to the almighty and infinitely awesome God from (out of or because of) His now-givens *(donis)*and past-givens *(datis)*--Christ, His Mother, the good angels, the saints on earth, as well as the saints in Heaven--who in various ways are *making* us to be *donis* or *memores,* and who are now fully *memores* through and in Christ.

Whom or what do all *memores* offer? *Hostiam puram, hostiam sanctam, hostiam immaculatam-- Panem sanctum vitae aeternae et Calicem salutis perpetuae.* All *memores* offer The Only Acceptable Victim for our sins. They offer the pure Victim, the holy Victim, the Immaculate Victim--the Holy Bread, Christ-crucified, the Source, Sustenance and Summit of eternal life; and, the Chalice, Christ-crucified, *Who* rendered us sinners saved from our natural and deserved destiny, Hell, for all eternity.

As a priest, Padre Pio brought the Mystery of Faith into his space-time. Most importantly, as a saint, he lived this Mystery of Faith, especially at Mass. He lived the Passion. He lived the Mass.

In saying his Canonized Mass from the Consecration up to Holy Communion, Padre Pio suffered with and *as* Christ--extreme abandonment and thirst. With Jesus, his inmost being was consumed by fire. He suffered with Christ and lived the Passion in order that he himself would become one of the Elect; and, to increase the number of the Elect, as well as, to increase his and their Heavenly glory.

THE IMMACULATA--HOSTIA IMMACULATA

Remember that somehow, as Simeon confirmed, Our Lady is *Hostia Immaculata*. Since Padre Pio was given the unseen stigmata (for the first seven years of his priesthood), how much more did Our Lady, in a similar unseen way--suffer for our sins? Indeed, as no one else other than Christ ever did or will, Our Lady prayed the Holy Mass, in all she did and in all that was done to her.

Make her sufferings effective unto salvation, your salvation and the salvation of others. As it were, the only disappointment or sorrow Our Lord and Our Lady have is the unrequitted love, the lack of eucharist or thanksgiving from those to whom they gave so very much, their very all. You can make up for this by being fully eucharist. Pray deeply and suffer greatly for yourself, sinners and others, and to console the two Hearts.

PRAY TO BE FULFILLED

*Supplices Te rogamus...ut quotquot... sumpserimus omni benedictione coelesti et gratia repleamur...*We beg of Thee, Almighty God...that the *quotquot* who receive Holy Communion may be filled with blessings from Heaven and all graces.

(Quotquot are defined in the Last Gospel. They received Christ and are now gestating in hope of being birthed into the eternal life of Heaven.) Participate in each Mass: not as a worldly and flesh-fixated sinner, but as one of the *quotquot* who is continually being born of (or gestated through) the Will of God--the Salutary Will of

God. You are called, and thereby blessed, to participate in the Heavenly Mystery. The Mystery of Faith is Christ's Saving Deed and Saving Person made present in our space-time as Christ instituted or decreed. With proper participation in Christ's Holy Sacrifice, you will be filled with graces and blessings.

This and this alone is the Mystery of the Catholic Faith. Merely professing that Christ died, is risen and will come again, as the mystery of faith, constitutes gross denial of the Christ-given and Catholic Mystery of Faith.

HUMBLY RECEIVE

At the climax of each Mass, as an unworthy sinner, you are allowed in certain circumstances to receive Christ on the tongue--Body, Blood, Soul and Divinity, under the appearance of bread. Be content with this awesome favor.

CHAPTER TWENTY-FOUR

FROM OBLATION TO DOXOLOGY

"The Holy Mass is a sacred union of Jesus and myself." (Padre Pio)

You are members of Jesus Christ (1 Cor 6, 15; 12, 27; Eph 5, 30). What an honor! But, also, what need for suffering this entails! When the Head is crowned with thorns, should the members be wearing a laurel of roses? When the Head is jeered and covered with mud from Calvary's road, should its members be enthroned and sprayed with perfume? When the Head has no pillow on which to rest, should its members be reclining on soft feathers? What an unheard of monster such a one would be! No, no, dear companions of the Cross, make no mistake. The Christians you see around you, fashionably attired, super-sensitive, excessively haughty and sedate, are neither true disciples nor true members of the Crucified Jesus...while blessing themselves with the Sign of the Cross, they crucify Jesus in their hearts.

If you are led by the spirit of Jesus and are living the same life with Him, your thorn-crowned head, then you must look forward to nothing but thorns, nails and lashes; in a word, to nothing but a cross.
(St. Louis De Montfort, a pre-cursor of the Fatima Message)

*Supra quae propitio ac sereno vultu respicere digneris...*Deign to look upon our oblations with a favorable and gracious countenance, and to accept our oblations as Thou didst accept the oblation of Thy just servant Abel, and the sacrifice of our Patriarch Abraham, and that which Thy high priest Melchisedech offered up to Thee, the Holy Sacrifice, the Immaculate Victim.

Again the priest, in praying the Holy Sacrifice, refers to (and prays over) your oblation, your being (or becoming) *Christ-ed*. He prays that such may come to be, and further, that it may be accepted by God. In this present year of Our Lord, your oblation, although *lumped with* that of

Abraham, Abel and Melchisedech, is different, yet much the same. Unlike Abel, Abraham and Melchisedech, you are in a year in which you know *how* Jesus is to be Master or Lord of your life. Now, *realize* this knowledge by being *Christ-ed,* through attending (or saying, if you are a priest) and then, living, the Holy Sacrifice of Mass.

Since Christ is God, He is Master and you are a servant--one who is to be oblated or sacrificed in His service. Your oblation is acceptable to God through Christ-suffering objectively; and through the application (as Trent defines the Mass) of Christ-suffering or Christ-crucified *in you.* However, your oblation is acceptable only as accomplished with the religious orientations (or mindsets) similar to those of Abel, Abraham and Melchisedech.

Let's briefly consider these mindsets which *by anticipation* allowed Abel, Abraham and Melchisedech to somehow be *Christ-ed*--to be taken into the Holy Sacrifice, *(Sanctum Sacrificium)* and to be made one with Christ-suffering, *Immaculatam Hostiam.*

JUST ABEL

One would think that Adam and his family would have learned the lesson--obey God or suffer--but Abel proved to be just, while Cain was unjust. *Just* in the Bible means *acceptable to God by doing what God wants,* as opposed to what one's flesh or the world wants.

God demanded animal sacrifice. Abel complied. Cain decided to give God what Cain thought best. Cain, (as do many today), *created God according to his own liking and subsequent imaginings.*

As it were, Cain's sin-trauma reverberates throughout the ages. Many go to Hell for not taking Jesus as He is--as demanding that we pray the Holy Sacrifice and that we eat His Flesh and drink His Blood. If you care for others, should you not remind your (non-Mass-attending) friends of their destiny for being disobedient to Jesus as revealed in His Holy Bible? The Holy Bible, the

Church and the saints assure us that the Mass was instituted by Christ. So teaches the Roman Catholic Church. (This point was paramount in The Liturgical Revolution, by Msgr. Klaus Gamber, which Cardinal Ratzinger approved in the original French edition). When considering the life of Padre Pio and the Mass that made Padre Pio, this point is awesome!

OBEDIENT ABRAHAM

You must become oblated to the extent that you achieve the depths of living in imitation of Abraham and his oblation. Let his mindset be yours. Abraham was willing to sacrifice his son-- the son of God's promises. How could he bring himself to do this? He trusted God. He trusted God--absolutely--without questioning and without reservation.

He believed in God so much that he knew God could raise children to him, even out of the dirt of the earth. Strive to imitate Abraham in his blind, total and trusting obedience to God's Holy Will.

At each Mass, does not God, as it were, raise Christ and the Elect out of mere bread and wine? Imitate Abraham. Trust God. Do all as Christ wills.

GOD'S PRIEST--MELCHISEDECH

The same Abraham acknowledged Melchisedech as God's priest. Melchisedech is a strange figure in history. He represents God's appointed priest-- somehow, both *one of* and *for* the people; and, *one from* and *with God*. As it were, he appears as the only true priest *in persona Christi*--yet only so by anticipation and type.

God makes priests as He desires. From His Revelation, we know that God despises people who claim to be priests. God despises all who think like Cain. God despises all church-bodies which create priests or allow priesthood to be exercised other than according to His Revealed Will as contained within Apostolic Tradition.

In this year of Our Lord, the only acceptable priests are those who have received valid Holy

Orders and who say valid Masses. Anyone else or anything else is an abomination in the sight of God. Only validly ordained priests saying valid Masses will bridge you to God and God to you. Each such pontifex or priest provides the Holy Sacrifice--your only hope of salvation from naturally inevitable Hell. Love, respect and obedience are due valid priests in this age of monumental Catholic and non-Catholic anti-clericalism--in this age within which anti-Christ reigns in the place of Christ.

FULL BLESSINGS

SUPPLICES te rogamus, omnipotens Deus: jube haec perferri per manus sancti Angeli tui in sublime altare tuum, in conspectu divinae majestatis tuae: ut quotquot ex hac altaris participatione, sacrosanctum Filii tui Corpus et Sanguinem sumpserimus, omni benedictione coelesti et gratia repleamur. Per eumdem Christum Dominum nostrum. Amen.

*With greatest humility, fear and reverence, we beg Thee, Almighty God, that **haec oblationes**--the offerings or oblations of us ordinary people, Thy **quotquot**, striving to be full and authentic oblations through and in Christ--may somehow be taken by Thy Holy Angels in the sight of Thy Divine Majesty, to Thine Holy Altar so that we **quotquot** who dare to receive the Body and Blood of Christ may be filled with graces and blessings from Heaven.*

We pray that our *Christ-ed* oblations (*haec oblationes*) be taken by the Holy Angel to God's Altar on high. We pray to the saints.

[They] fell down before the Lamb... incense mingles with the prayers of the saints (Apoc 5:8) saying 'Worthy is the Lamb that was slain to receive all power, riches, honor and glory' (Apoc 5:12).

Interestingly, we are referred to Apocalypse 8-12 by those who read the Third Revelation of

Fatima. Chapter eight begins as follows.

> I saw the Angel who came and stood at
> the Altar with a golden censer. Incense
> was given to him. He offered the prayers
> of all the saints upon the golden altar
> before the very Throne of God. The
> smoke of incense mingled with the
> prayers of the saints and ascended up
> before God out of the Angel's hand
> (Apoc 8:3-4).

PERTINENT NEGATIVE OBSERVATION

We have been taken up into the imagery of the
smoke or incense rising before the Throne of God.
The Mass allows those of us who are saints to be
part of that most holy incense or smoke.

Descending from the sublime to the sacrilegious,
let's consider another pertinent incense
observation. This observation was made by a
modern pope. Let's listen to this pope and profit
by his wisdom. Pope Paul VI was fond of
repeating: *"The smoke of Satan has entered the*

sanctuary of the Catholic Church." This was the pope who--contrary to the wishes of Vatican II, of the perennial *sensus et praxis fidelium,* of the majority of bishops; and, of Apostolic and Church Tradition--allowed to be used many similarly themed, but different, nationally fabricated liturgies.

Indeed, this papal observation is revealing. In the light of our reflections on the incense or smoke that should ascend to God mingled with the oblations of the saints, Pope Paul VI seems to indicate that Satan is being worshipped in the existential Catholic Church. Was he right?

PRAYING FOR THOSE IN PURGATORY

Memento etiam, Domine, famulorum famulorumquetuarum...Memento--bring into the full realization of the Memory, O Lord, Thy servants and handmaids N... and N...who are gone before us with an indication or sign of being in the faith and who sleep the sleep of peace. To these, O Lord, and to all who rest in

Christ, grant we beseech Thee, that
place of refreshment, light and peace.

First of all, we cannot pray for the damned. Therefore, we pray for those who apparently lived and died in the Catholic Faith. We pray that their Purgatory be alleviated. Purgatory is most real. If you love anyone, you will pray for their salvation from Hell and the mercy of God toward them in the most awful purifying fires of Purgatory.

Here, at the Saving Event, pray for those who have left us with the sign of being part of the Elect. Pray for them. They beg for your Mass prayers. Here is a most important community concern--to pray for the Church suffering--to pray for the poor souls in Purgatory.

As you come to a far deeper faith or even to truly believe, then, you'll be led to live *positively* to Christ-crucified. You will live ever more dead to your flesh and to the world--the opinions, validations, praises, opinions etc. of the community or of another human being. You will live more fully, and more sensitively obedient to God's Will.

242

You will realize that it is far better to be purged now, than to be purged in Purgatory (if, of course, you are one of the Elect). Your vision will be vertical--towards God and the spiritual--and no longer horizontal, toward man and this world.

You might avoid reality for a time. You may live to *love man as he is in order to create the perfect world here on earth.* However, reality will win out. Reality will either transform you or it will burn you eternally. Why not be transformed as Christ demands? Why go to Hell out of love for the flesh and this world?

Certainly, regarding this topic, we can all learn from Padre Pio. He was harsh in the confessional. He was truly *in persona Christi.* He realized his flesh was his enemy. He loved not this world or the people of this world. He loved Christ totally and exclusively. Then, out of and because of such love, he related to or cared for others as God wished him to do so.

Padre Pio was so much of a true priest that no modern bishop in the USA would be able to endure the likes of him for any length of time. For example, what bishop would tolerate a priest who annoyed the people by taking three hours to say Mass? Or, what bishop or congregation would tolerate a priest who said *only* the Canonized Mass? Or, what bishop could survive, and much less overcome, the onslaught of complaints from penitents who were treated harshly, sternly and non-complimentarily by that great confessor, Padre Pio?

NOBIS QUOQUE PECCATORIBUS

Paradoxically, one of the signs of sainthood, is that great saints realize that they themselves are great sinners. And so did St. Louis De Montfort as he wrote:

> All of you are sinners and there is not a single one who is not deserving of Hell; I myself deserve it the most. These sins of ours must be punished either here or hereafter. If they are punished in this world, they will not be punished in the world to come.

If we agree to God's punishing here below, this punishment will be dictated by love. For mercy, which holds sway in this world, will mete out the punishment, and not strict justice. This punishment will be light and momentary, blended with merit and sweetness and followed up with reward both in time and eternity.

However, if the punishment due to our sins is held over for the next world, then God's avenging justice, which means fire and blood, will see to the punishing. What horrible punishment! How incomprehensible, how unspeakable! 'Who knoweth the power of Thy anger?' (Ps 89,11).

Punishment devoid of mercy (James 1,13), pity, mitigation or merit; without limit and without end. Yes, without end! That mortal sin of a moment that you committed, that deliberate evil thought which now escapes your memory, the word that is gone with the wind, that act of such short duration against God's law--they shall all be punished for an eternity, punished with the devils of Hell, as long as God is God!

The God of vengeance will have no pity on your torments or your sobs and tears, violent enough to cleave the rocks. Suffering and still more suffering, without merit, without mercy and without end! (St. Louis De Montfort)

*Nobis quoque peccatoribus--to us, sinners, also...*Padre Pio struck his breast with such conviction that the thump could be heard throughout the chapel. Only one human person is sinless. She who defined her unique identity: *"I am the Immaculate Conception."* She is *Immaculata*--from the beginning of her life to the very end and thus, forever. Nothing in her--from the past, in the present or in the future is, was or will be sin. Sin is the only real evil since only sin brings one into the eternal fires of Hell. To us, sinners, grant bountiful pardon for our sins. Paradoxically, even when one's sins have been forgiven, he is still defined as a sinner. Only one human person is *Immaculata.*

God is merciful and just. You will be damned to eternal Hell because you never sincerely or sufficiently repented of your sins and sincerely sought God's forgiveness on His terms. You have the opportunity of Heaven because of God's mercy or loving-kindness. However, God cannot forgive (and thus take into Heaven) one who won't confess his need for forgiveness. Likewise, Holy Mary only accepts as her children those who are humble enough to petition her: *"Holy Mary, Mother of God, pray for us **sinners**."*

Perhaps, you still reject His terms for salvation-- e.g., going to a priest for confession of mortal sins in order to have such sins forgiven. Perhaps, you are a hardened victim of new age heresy, deciding what is to be good or evil; to be true or false. Perhaps, you join the sinners who reject one or more fundamentals of God's Natural Law--e.g. that premarital sex or the use of contraceptives is matter for mortal sin. If you are, guess who will win at God's judgment? In your imagination, you may escape reality, but never so in the real world.

How can one be saved from the effects of sin who is too proud to admit that he is a gross sinner--a sinner by birth and inclination; a sinner in deed and in habit? How can such a sinner be saved from Hell?

THE DOXOLOGY PART ONE

Per quem haec omnia, Domine, semper bona creas, sanctificas, vivificas, benedicis, et praestas nobis...By Whom, O Lord, Thou dost always create, sanctify, bring back to life, bless and bestow upon us, the Elect, all that is for our good.

This prayer unites with the next to form the Elect's Divine Praise. Thus, do the Elect acknowledge Christ as God's link with His Elect ones. Christ is the priest or pontifex for the Elect. All that is good for the Elect comes from Christ. All that is for God's positive external glory from His Elect comes through, with and in Christ. The Eastern Liturgy has a similar doxology: *"All of what is Thine, we give to Thee in all (we do) and for the sake of (Thine) all."*

THE DOXOLOGY PART TWO

Per ipsum, et cum ipso, et in ipso, est tibi Deo Patri omnipotenti, in unitate Spiritus Sancti, omnis honor, et gloria. Through Him and with Him, and in Him, is unto Thee, God the Father Almighty, in the unity of the Holy Ghost, all honor and glory.

In the second part of the doxology we confess that any and all honor and glory--any and all external rational thanksgivings and praises of God's attributes--come to God through Jesus Christ. Through Him, with Him, and in Him, any and all glory and honor goes to God. Heaven for us humans is praising, thanking and honoring Christ-Crucified for having made us into His Memory and for Christ being Who He is (Apoc 5:4).

Worthy is the Lamb that was slain to receive the Elect's thanksgiving and praise forever and ever.

Heaven for us humans who will be part of the Elect is praising and thanking God forever for the Saving Deed and the Saving Person--for the Mass and Christ, Holy Eucharist. As it were, start or pre-figure Heaven by praising and thanking God for each Mass you attend and for every visit you make to Christ, Holy Eucharist.

All souls will glorify God. Every knee in Hell will acknowledge God for His justice! Every one of the eternally damned will glorify God's justice.

That's a most needed message for this perverse generation which lives and breathes presumption. In spite of current demonic belief, you aren't necessarily, or even easily, saved from eternal Hell. You are here to choose--to agonizingly obey Christ and then go to Heaven or not to do so and go to eternal Hell. Either way, you glorify God-- His loving-kindness or His perfect justice. God wins whether you go to Heaven or go to Hell forever and ever.

That's part of the mystery of God's Salutary Plan-

-that your temporal free moral choices will determine the eternal mode of your existence. What an awesome, frightening and sobering realization for those who live for or from others or their own flesh. Therefore, agonize to take advantage of the opportunity--to embrace and love the Mass, both as Sacrifice and in its fruit-- the Sacrament of the Holy Eucharist. Pray the Mass as Padre Pio did. Live the Mass as Padre Pio did.

Work out your salvation most carefully. How can you escape eternal Hell if you neglect to appreciate and love the Mystery of Faith? Appreciate and love the Mass to such an extent that you let the Mass that made Padre Pio, make you into one of the Elect.

CHAPTER TWENTY-FIVE

PRAYER TO THE FATHER

Our Father, Who art in heaven, hallowed be Thy Name. Thy kingdom come; Thy Will be done on earth as it is in heaven.

How dare we mere and sinful humans address the eternal and omnipotent God as Father? Yet, Jesus commanded us to do so in order to be saved from Hell.

We hallow or glorify God in a positive way by going to Heaven. We agree that Thy Name be hallowed by all--the unjust in eternal Hell showing forth Thy justice and the few in Heaven showing forth Thy mercy and love.

May Thy kingdom come to us now--in the Saving Deed and the Saving Person, constituting Heaven itself. May this kingdom be here for me and mine as we pray the Canonized Mass to be delivered by Thy Saving Deed and as we commune with the Saving Person. Thy kingdom come. May I have the Blessing for me and mine both now and eternally.

Thy Saving Will be done on earth as it is done in Heaven. May Thy Canonized Mass always be with us--on earth as it is in Heaven. All of the Church Fathers predicted that there will come a time when this Holy Sacrifice will (almost totally) be absent from our earth. May the Canonized Mass be restored as the one and only *par*. May Thy Saving Will be once more done as Thou willest it to be done; as it is done in Heaven, where the Lamb Once Slain--the Holy Sacrifice-- defines Heaven for the Elect.

Give Jesus Thy Son to us every day in Holy Communion. Here is our greatest blessing--the Holy Sacrifice of Mass and Jesus, Holy Sacrament. May we always have this Blessing.

Forgive us as we forgave our fellow men (as the original Aramaic states). God actively forgives as God. We, mere humans, can forgive in the past tense--by letting go of, or by giving up hatred and/or love for any and all creatures (persons, places or things). Guide, guard and grace us from sin and deliver us from Satan's kingdom. Sin is the only present evil. Hell is the only eternal evil.

From both of these, we ask God the Father's deliverance. The only way of deliverance is The Saving Deed and the Saving Person. As Christ began our prayer, so He ends it. The only way to be delivered from our natural destiny--Satan's kingdom on earth from and into Hell eternal--is through God the Father's blessing--His kingdom made present on earth from and into Heaven eternal. Amen.

LIBERA NOS DOMINE

Deliver us, we beseech Thee, O Lord, from all evils, past, present and to come, and by the intercession of the Blessed and glorious ever Virgin Mary, Mother of God, together with Thy blessed apostles Peter and Paul, Andrew, and all the saints, mercifully grant peace in our days, that through the bounteous help of Thy mercy we may be always free from sin, and safe from all disquiet.

Pray to God that by your proper prayers, mortifications and restitutions, God's purifying and purgatorial punishments for your past evils--your past insufficiently dealt with sins--may be lessened. Also, pray for God's freely given forgiveness of these sins--that none of them may put you into Hell.

Pray the Holy Mass--that the salutary graces of this Mass may apply to you: to lead you to repent and properly confess your past sins; to do penance for them; to be graced in the present--this day or this week or until the next Mass you attend; to be freed from or to avoid present and future sins; and finally, that your future in eternity may be free from the only eternal evil--Hell.

Free us, O Lord, from all evils--past, present and to come. *Libera nos a malo.*

DELIVER US FROM THE EFFECTS OF OUR SINS AND GIVE US PEACE

After the Pater Noster, the celebrant takes the paten--placed at the right under the corporal. He holds it in a vertical position as he says the prayer, *Deliver us*.

The paten is a symbol of peace. At the words, *Vouchsafe us your peace*, he kisses the paten and makes over himself a large sign of the cross, since the cross is the Source of True Peace.

He next places the Sacred Host on the paten. From this moment, the paten becomes not only the sign of peace, but its throne. Only when Christ is King will man enjoy true and lasting peace.

CHAPTER TWENTY-SIX

THE CULMINATION POINT

Holy Communion was the culminating point of Padre Pio's [Canonized] Mass. It was both the supreme moment of participating in the passion and of enjoying the Divine Embrace of Christ Glorified. (Padre Pio's Mass, Fr. Tarcisco, San Giovanni Rotondo, 1992, pp 46-50)

Lamb of God, Who takest away the sins of the world, have mercy on us.

Day of wrath, that inevitable day of God's Judgment...Who for me will be interceding when decent people will be in dire need of mercy?

O good Jesus, please remember that I am the reason for Thy coming to be. Be, then, my Saviour. Lamb of God, have mercy on me!

We who live far below the spiritual level of Padre

257

Pio, primarily receive Jesus in order to be graced into not going to eternal Hell. However, as we do so, we confess our awesome unworthiness.

> *Domine, non sum dignus, ut intres sub tectum meum: sed tantum dic verbo, et sanabitur anima mea.*

> *Lord, I am not worthy that Thou shouldst come under my roof, but only say the word and my soul shall be healed.*

Let Christ live in you to help make you *worthy* or *less unworthy* of receiving Him. Let Christ live in you to conform you to Christ Crucified.

CHRIST TODAY

The Holy Ghost doesn't brood over humanity or over the whole world. He broods only over the Elect--to actualize the full number of the Elect. The Holy Ghost does this in a special way at each Canonized Mass--especially in Holy Communion. In these precious moments as Christ communes, the Holy Ghost broods.

Here at each valid Mass is the Source of the Elect's solitary power to be what they are. Here is the Mystery of Faith--Christ's Saving Will realized once again in our space-time in an infinitely awesome way. Let your Holy Communion fill you with graces and blessings. Let Holy Communion be a time of *love*--loving Christ with all of your mind, heart and soul.

Let Holy Communion be a time of *realistic love*. The power or grace to become one of the few, one of the Elect, is given to the *quotquot*--to those who believe in Jesus Christ (Jn 1) and therefore believe in the *semper et ubique idem* Catholic Church. Graces come to the *quotquot* as they receive the power and Person of Christ in order to die to their flesh, their earthly heritage and to the world; and to live according to God's Revealed Will.   Even as we are blessed to receive Christ Glorified, we do so as those whose only challenge is to become or to live Christ Crucified.

CHRIST'S ALTAR OF SACRIFICE

In a special way, during Communion, your body becomes an altar--*an altar of sacrifice.* St. Leonard of Port Maurice observed:

> The Altar is surrounded with angels adoring the Real Presence of Jesus Christ, adding their praise and worship with ours. (The Hidden Treasure)

Join the angels and saints adoring Christ, Holy Eucharist. Ever strive to become the altar of Christ's Sacrifice.

Padre Pio's Holy Communion *didn't* lead him to *space out into self-glorifying ecstasy.* His favorite image for Holy Communion related him to his own *final* Holy Communion--his being taken down from *the altar of sacrifice.* For our saint, the *Pieta* was the *logon* of Holy Communion.

Padre Pio disclosed to us a great mystery: Die *with* and *in Christ* in order to be received into the arms of Mary, Our Mother by Christ's gift at Calvary: "Son, behold your mother."

Having Christ come to *live within oneself in order to die within oneself* demands one's passion unto death in and into Christ Crucified. Whenever Christ lives in any person this side of death He lives in that body and soul as He lived in His own human nature, to die to the flesh and the world, and to live God the Father's Will; or (in other words) unto His Salutary Passion and Death.

Padre Pio's advice to Holy Communicants: "Ask to be another Jesus." Do you really want to commune *with* and *into* Jesus as described above? If you do, then you will receive Holy Communion with great love and a new awareness--the awareness which led Padre Pio to become an altar of Christ's *Sacrifice*.

From now on, strive to receive Christ with a greater awareness of what is happening and what you are doing. Once again, recall Padre Pio's mystical understanding of receiving Holy Communion. Has not the stigmatist-priest opened up to us a deeper meaning for Holy Communion--a meaning which enlivens and applies the *Pieta* to you and me? For our bodies to be received into the loving arms of Our Lady, they must be like unto Christ's Body--the Altar upon which Christ's Blood was shed. For our bodies to be like unto Christ's Body, we must be *crucified in and into* Christ.

CHAPTER TWENTY-SEVEN

PADRE PIO'S FAVORITE PRAYER

In the beginning was the Word and the Word was with God; and the Word was God. He was in the beginning with God. All things were made through Him, and without Him was made nothing that has been made. In Him was life, and the life was the light of men. And the light shines in the darkness; and the darkness grasped it not. There was a man, sent from God, whose name was John. This man came as a witness, to give testimony of the Light, that all might believe through Him. He was not himself the Light, but was to bear witness to the Light. It was the true Light that enlightens every man who comes into the world. He was in the world, and the world was made by Him, but the world knew Him not. He came unto His own, and His own received Him not. But to as many as received Him, quotquot, He gave the power of becoming sons of God; to those who believe in His name:

who were born not of blood, nor of the will of the flesh, nor of the will of man, but of God. And the Word was made flesh and dwelt among us. And we saw His glory, the glory as of the Only-begotten of the Father, full of grace and truth.

Padre Pio was especially impressed and highly motivated by the last gospel. He was *in love with the last gospel*. Let us see why and how this is true.

The last gospel is a revelation about God--about His tremendous love for us. God so loved mankind that He gave each human being the chance to be saved from Hell. The Last Gospel records mankind's reaction to God's Gift. It discloses the actual truth about men and their attainment of salvation from Hell. Many, not few, go to eternal Hell.

The Last Gospel discloses the ugly reality of who man really is. Man is a wretched sinner by birth, by tendency, in deed and in habit. Man in his pride naturally opts for darkness to exalt himself as if he were a god. Only a very few are saved from *man the sinner's* natural destiny or definition--Hell (as Limbo or as Hell-Hell). Naturally, or in his unredeemed nature, each (except for Our Lady) is Hell-bound. Following one's naturally ungraced conscience and whatever religion one thinks is best will lead such natural men into eternal Hell--not to Heaven as contemporary deception preaches.

Through the Word, the Second Person of the Holy Trinity, all was made. Adam *for and in* his progeny rejected the Light. He disobeyed God's simple command. Thus, he sinned for himself and for his progeny.

Then, in God's right time, the Word became flesh (assumed a human nature). He came unto the world of men who were made by Him. In general, men rejected their Creator-Redeemer. He came unto His special people--those who were prepared by Him for His coming for over a thousand years. In general, they refused to recognize and accept Him as their Messiah.

At this point, Padre Pio wept. He wept in joy realizing the infinite love of God. He wept in sorrow realizing the great sinfulness of men.

THE QUOTQUOT

However, a few--the *quotquot*--accepted Christ as Messiah and as Saviour from sin and became Catholics. To these, Christ gave the potential to become children of God and to be freed from being Hell-bound (Hell as limbo or as Hell-Hell).

The *quotquot* are the potentially Heaven-born. They are in *gestation*. They truly and fully believed in Jesus. They became Catholics in truth and in spirit; and were validly baptized into Catholicism. Some, not all, *quotquot* will be gestated as God demands. These will be born into eternal Heaven. What is this *gestation as God demands?* To be properly gestated, one must be gestated (or now live) by being born--*not* by blood; *not* by the Flesh; and *not* by the world, but by obedience to *God as Revealed*. Salutary birth-- final gestation into Heaven--cannot occur through

Padre Pio Drawing: Barbara Kellam

blood, through pride of life-origin, as being blood-born as a Jew, an American, a Black or whatever else. Such life-force of gestation is abortifacient unto eternal life in Heaven.

Birth into Heaven cannot occur by being nourished by the world--by living for or from another man, one's spouse, one's lover, one's boss, one's child, one's subject, one's friend, etc. One cannot please God and man; nor, can one live for (or from) his own flesh and please God. Such perverted gestating is lethal. It will birth one into Hell (as a Hell of eternal pains).

Transferring analogies, each must agonizingly walk the path to salvation--salvation as spelled out by *God as revealed.* One must die to his flesh and to this world. One must live for (or from) *God as revealed.* One must become a Catholic, in truth and in spirit, and one must die (or be birthed) as an authentic *mortal sin free* Catholic to be born into the eternal life of Heaven (that is, after Pentecost, of course).

It must be regretfully acknowledged that many

who claim to be Catholics aren't--according to surveys and reliable studies. An overwhelming majority of them are gross heretics. As such, they are infinitely worse off than those who have never united to the quotquot (presuming, of course, that their baptisms were administered validly--not with a positively contrary intention to having original sin removed).

COLOSSIANS' MYSTERY

This is how Padre Pio read the Last Gospel. It grieved him. This grief led him to do all he could to help save souls from the eternal fires of Hell.

This Last Gospel motivated Padre Pio to become more conformed to Christ the Saviour, so as to bring more graces to Hell-bound sinners so that many of the quotquot would be led to convert and thus attain Heaven. This Gospel motivated Padre Pio to properly love men in the only way possible through his saying, praying, and living the Holy Sacrifice of the Mass.

This Last Gospel inspired Padre Pio to live the Mass by suffering with and in Christ--to live the Colossians' Mystery.

> It is my joy, my life, to suffer for the sake of building up Christ's Body the Church. I strive to complete what is lacking of Christ's [desired] sufferings in my body, for the sake of His Body, the Church (Col 1:25).

LAST LETTER TO THE POPE

One of the last things that Padre Pio did was to write a letter to Pope Paul VI, in which he stated:

> I offer you my prayers and daily sufferings as a small but sincere contribution on the part of the least of your sons, in order that God may lead you with His grace to follow the straight and painful path in defense of *eternal truth, which does not change with the passing of the years.* (Padre Pio, Letter to Pope Paul VI)

Ten days later, the only stigmatist-priest in the history of the Church, died. In a similar way, we now pray for the present pope that he may follow the straight and painful path in defense of eternal truth--especially, of the eternal truth of the Canonized Mass of the Latin Rite, the Mass that made Padre Pio to be who he was and who he will be for all eternity, the Saint of the Canonized Mass.

Recall that unique mystery and secret which Padre Pio disclosed to us. **Die *with* and *in* Christ, in order to be received into the arms of Mary.**

May the Pieta apply to you. May Holy Mary, Mother of God, receive you--*dead in Christ*--into her arms, both now and at the hour of your death. Amen.

CHAPTER TWENTY-EIGHT

OUR GLORIOUS FUTURE

We are not foolish optimists who commit the gross sin of presumption. We suffer with Christ in this age of the Fatima Curse, when because of our sinfulness, the Mass that made Padre Pio is being eclipsed or even taken away from us. However, we do not despair.

We know that one day and season the Mass that made Padre Pio *will be restored.* The Mass that made Padre Pio a saint *will be restored.*

History repeats itself. The Fatima Message, other authentic Marian apparitions, predictions by saints and all of Biblical prophecy exhibit a consistent pattern: a rotten church with only a few God-pleasing members. There follow chastisements, which then usher in a reformed church and many blessings.

St. John Bosco is famous for his vision and prophecies. His vision concerned the heavily assailed ship representing the existential church with a truly Marian pope guiding it between two pillars, one for the Holy Eucharist and the other for Our Lady. This vision occurred in January 1870. (I Sogni di Don Bosco, Turin, or THE MEMOIRES as translated in Catholic Counter-Reformation November and December 1993)

St. John Bosco's two pillars reflect God's Fatima Message. In 1916, the children of Fatima were led to adore the Holy Eucharist. *Then*, Our Lady appeared in 1917. These are the God-given Pillars of Salvation in our day.

Indeed, Our Lady of Fatima and every authentic Church-approved Marian apparition is a visit from Our Lady of the Holy Sacrifice and Holy Sacrament, or Our Lady of the Canonized Mass-- as we have seen. Certainly, Our Lady, the Holy Sacrifice and the Holy Sacrament are inseparable.

According to the *rules for prophecy-validation*, the *short term* or immediate prophecy of Bosco concerning the fate of France was precisely validated within the next five years. Thus, the remote prophecy--which, is being fulfilled at present--was proven to be reliable.

Bosco's end-times prophecy is written in <u>THE MEMOIRES</u>. This prophecy warns of tribulations. It predicts victory for a reformed or converted pope--a pope who finally comes to fully obey and please God and to *de-focus* on man and the here and now.

ECCLESIAL ECLIPSE

The ecclesial eclipse when (in the words of La Salette) Rome will lose the Faith and become the seat of anit-Christ, has been predicted and even confirmed by popes. Nearly a century ago, (in preparation for Evangelization 1900) Pope Leo XIII had a vision of Satan's ecclesial victories. This vision led him to compose his Leonine Prayer. Pope Leo explains the reason for his prayer:

> In the Holy Place itself, where has been set up the See of the most holy Peter and the Chair of Truth for the Light of the world, they have raised the throne of their abominable impiety, with the iniquitous design that when the Pastor

has been struck, the sheep may be scattered. (THE RACCOLTA, 1930, Benziger Bros., pages 314, 315)

Pope Pius XII, according to Msgr. Roche, writing in Pie devant l'histoire, dreaded the coming of a bad pope:

> A day will come when the civilized world will deny its God, WHEN THE CHURCH WILL DOUBT, as Peter doubted. She will be tempted to believe THAT MAN HAS BECOME GOD...IN OUR CHURCHES CHRISTIANS WILL SEARCH IN VAIN FOR THE RED LAMP WHERE GOD AWAITS THEM. Like Magdalen weeping before the EMPTY TOMB, they will ask 'WHERE HAVE THEY taken Him?' (Pope Pius XII, Pie XII devant l'histoire", Msgr. Roche, pp. 52-53, caps added).

Pope Paul VI observed that the smoke of Satan had entered the *sanctuary of the Church.* Sanctuary smoke is smoke of worship. Was Pope Paul VI honestly commenting on his own *abominable desolation*--the unholy in the place of

The Holy?

At the beginning of his pontificate, Pope John Paul II met with the German bishops at Fulda. They persisted in attempting to uncover the Third Revelation of Fatima, which was kept secret by papal command. Pope John Paul evaded the question. Finally, he urged them: *"Pray the rosary. Pray the rosary."*

This reminds us of a prophecy given by Our Lady of Fatima that a time will come when "all that will be left is *the rosary and devotion to my Immaculate Heart."*

Certainly, this *implies* that there will be no more Masses. Could this be true? *All of the Fathers of the Church have predicted that there will come a period within which (in general, at least) the Holy Sacrifice will cease.*

In the light of these papal prophecies and confirmations, St. John Bosco's prophecy is even more foreboding:

Your sons ask for bread of faith and no one gives it to them...Ungrateful Rome, effeminate Rome, arrogant Rome...forgetting that the Sovereign Pontiff's and your true glory are on Golgotha...Woe to you. My LAW is an idle word for you. (THE MEMOIRES, St. John Bosco).

CONVERTED POPE BLESSED CHURCH

Today, it is the Catholic Church herself that is under attack. In her functions, in her sacred institutions, in her Head, in her doctrine and in her discipline, she is assailed as Catholic Church, as centre of the truth, as mistress of all the faithful.

And it is to merit Heaven's special protection that we have recourse to Mary, as the Mother of us all, as the special help of Catholic kings and peoples, of Catholics all over the world. (St. John Bosco, Wonders of the Mother of God, Turn, 1868, p.7).

As at Fatima, St. John Bosco assures us that victory will be attained through Our Lady. She will win for her pope the graces to return to *properly and plenarily pope-ing.*

In Bosco's vision, a reformed or converted pope and his small band gradually increase in numbers. This authentically Marian pope will enter St. Peter's to celebrate the Canonized Mass. The angels rejoice as at Bethlehem, some two thousand years ago. These angels join the pope in the *Gloria* of the Mass. Heaven rejoices as peace through the Canonized Mass is brought back to men of good will. *"The world will see an era of peace,"* says Our Lady of Fatima.

> When he [the pope] entered the holy city, he began to weep over the desolation of its inhabitants, many of whom were no more. Then, entering St. Peter's, he intoned the Te Deum, which was followed by a choir of angels singing *'Gloria in excelsis Deo, et in terra pax hominibus bonae voluntatis.'*
> (THE MEMOIRES, St. John Bosco)

Subsequently, this Marian pope, taking the advice given long ago by Pope St. Pius X, sees the enemy--the reigning experts and authorities. He fires them. Then he appoints as counsel two saintly advisors. This Marian pope is soon rewarded for his decisiveness and fidelity:

> At that moment, two angels could be seen presenting the Pope with a standard and saying to him: 'Receive this banner from Him Who fights and scatters the most powerful armies of the earth. Your enemies have fled and your sons are imploring you with sighs and tears...' On the standard was written: 'REGINA SINE LABE CONCEPTA,' and on the other side: 'AUXILIUM CHRISTIANORUM [of Catholics].'
> (THE MEMOIRES, St. John Bosco)

The Immaculata repares the existential church through Christ. Christ repares the existential church through the restoration of the Holy Sacrifice of the Mass. Our Lady of these end-times is Our Lady of the Canonized Mass. The Immaculata, the Help of Catholics, will restore the Canonized Mass.

The enemy knows for certain that this Mass is the LIFE and POWER of the Church on earth. *"Tolle Missam, tolle ecclesiam."* This was the arch-heretic Luther's motto for battle. This is the motto for conquest of contemporary apostates-within.

Restore the Mass and major heresies evaporate. Our Lady of the Canonized Mass will do this. She will restore our LIFE and POWER. St. John Bosco sees that Our Lady will restore the par: **"She clothes the venerable Old Man in all former vestments."** (*Former vestments* are the discarded papal and priestly vestments). Once again, the pope will *pope* and *be priest* as God demands.

Through the Canonized Mass, this pope, restored to *properly and plenarily pope-ing*, will conquer all of the errors prevalent in today's church:

> Though difficulties remain, they will be resolved. If you find yourself in difficulty, do not stop but carry on until

the hydra head of error is broken. This blow will cause earth and hell to tremble...The Pope will reign as before. It will be a terrible hour for evil and for Hell...But the world will be reassured, and the good will rejoice. (THE MEMOIRES)

The old order will be restored. Error and heresy will be annihilated. The Church will be brought back to *par*:

> When a foulness invades the whole Church...we must return to the Church of the past. (THE HIDDEN TREASURE, St. Leonard)

THE HEAVENLY RAINBOW OF PEACE

> BEHOLD the heavenly rainbow, pacifying the storms of Divine Justice! For myself, I believe that, were it not for the Holy Mass, at this present moment, the world would be in the abyss, unable to bear up under the mighty load of its iniquities. (St. Vincent of Lerins)

281

When will the *Bosco and Fatima* promised *era of peace* materialize? When will the *rainbow of peace* once again envelope and refresh the Church with peace? Listen to St. John Bosco:

> Iniquity is consummated: sin has come to an end and, before the two full moons of the month of the flowers have passed, THE RAINBOW OF PEACE will appear over the earth. (The Memoires, St. John Bosco)

Abbe de Nantes has calculated that the only month of flowers (March, in Italy) that has two full moons will be: MARCH--1999. By that time, will ecclesial reparation have been accomplished? In that day (of ecclesial reparation), we will live under the rainbow of peace *in* the Canonized Liturgy.

A rainbow of peace appeared in Silver Springs, Nevada, in 1990. This rainbow enveloped the "traditionalist church"--a church which was, at that very hour being dedicated to exclusive celebration of the Canonized Mass. Perhaps, this miraculous rainbow was a portent of *the* rainbow of peace. [See my book PRAY THE HOLY MASS. This event was captured on video.]

In the *mean*time, pray and sacrifice. Live as St. Vincent of Lerins counselled--by returning to *the Church of the past.* If nothing else, your attending the Canonized Mass will raise the questions or problems which in turn--as happened throughout Church history--will call forth a *dogmatic* council.

Trent II or its equivalent will be brought about by the actions of those who are militantly faithful. Your attendance and your enthusiastic dedication to the Canonized Mass of the Latin Rite of the Catholic Church will help bring about MARIAN ECCLESIAL REPARATION or the restoration of Catholicism.

How great will be this restored church? It will be as the Great Proven Miracle of Fatima predicted. The sun (the Church) will be repared and function as God expects it to function.

THE SUN REPARED

On October 13, 1917, in Fatima, everyone saw the sun--representing the existential church--being not only totally dysfunctional but also a grave menace to mankind. Then, Our Lady restored the sun to its par or to functioning properly.

The *sun*, representing the existential church, was *aberrant* and dysfunctional. It left its appointed orbit or function, it pleased men with various colorations, and finally, it became so dysfunctional, it became the scourge of mankind and was about to destroy all mankind. Then, Our Lady of the Canonized Mass, THE IMMACULATA, by the power given to her by God, restored or repared the existential church.

Indeed, as Fatima disclosed, Our Lady is God's freely chosen prime end-times Sacramental. Through her, ecclesial reparation will materialize. The sun will become brighter than ever before. Padre Pio is a glimpse into this glorious future. The Mass that made Padre Pio a saint will make many like unto him, once ecclesial reparation occurs.

The sun was repared. Within the rainbow of peace, the Church will be repared. As Fatima promises and as John Bosco confirms, this sun will shine so brightly that it will convert Russia to Catholicism and will bring peace to the whole world:

> Over the whole world there will appear a sun as bright as the flames of the cenacle, such as will never be seen from that time until the end of time. (THE MEMOIRES, St. John Bosco)

Padre Pio, Saint of the Canonized Mass, pray for us. Pray that the Mass that made you, will once again flourish in our midst. Pray that we will be blessed with many priests such as you were.

Other Books by Fr. Paul Trinchard

ALL ABOUT SALVATION

APOSTASY WITHIN

GOD'S WORD

HOLY MARY HOLY MASS

MY BASIC MISSAL

NEW AGE NEW MASS

NEW MASS IN LIGHT OF THE OLD

PRAY THE HOLY MASS

RUSSIA'S ERROR

THE AWESOME FATIMA
CONSECRATIONS

THE ABBOT ON LITURGY

THE QUESTION & ANSWER BOOK on liturgy